# THE UNIVERSE AT LARGE

HERMANN BONDI, Professor of Applied Mathematics, King's College, University of London, was born in Vienna in 1919. Educated at Trinity College, Cambridge (B.A., 1940; M.A., 1944), he was, until 1954, a Fellow of the College and Lecturer in Mathematics at Cambridge. He has been, in addition, a Research Associate at Cornell (1951) and at the Harvard College Observatory (1953). Professor Bondi has done research principally in the areas of the composition of stars and interstellar space, cosmology, and geophysics. Author of *Cosmology,* Professor Bondi has written for *Discovery* and *Reviews of Modern Physics* and has been a regular contributor to the Monthly Notices of the Royal Astronomical Society. He lives with his wife and five young children on Reigate Heath, Surrey, England.

Hermann Bondi, Professor of Applied Mathematics, King's College, University of London, was born in Vienna in 1919. Educated at Trinity College, Cambridge (B.A., 1940; M.A., 1944), he was, until 1954, Fellow of the College and Lecturer in Mathematics at Cambridge. He has been, in addition, a Research Associate at Cornell (1951) and at the University of Chicago (1953). Professor Bondi has done research principally in the areas of the composition of stars and interstellar space, cosmology, and geophysics. Author of Cosmology, Professor Bondi has written for television and radio and Mr. Bondi has often been a regular contributor to the monthly science of the Royal Astronomical Society. He lives with his wife and five young children at Reigate Heath, Surrey, England.

# THE UNIVERSE AT LARGE

Hermann Bondi

SCIENCE
STUDY
SERIES

Published by
Anchor Books
Doubleday & Company, Inc.
Garden City, New York

ILLUSTRATIONS BY PERCY H. LUND

*Library of Congress Catalog Card Number 60–13501*

*Copyright © 1960 by Educational Services Incorporated*
*Copyright © 1959, 1960 by The Illustrated London News*
*All Rights Reserved*
*Printed in the United States of America*

# THE SCIENCE STUDY SERIES

The Science Study Series offers to students and to the general public the writing of distinguished authors on the most stirring and fundamental topics of science, from the smallest known particles to the whole universe. Some of the books tell of the role of physics in the world of man, his technology and civilization. Others are biographical in nature, telling the fascinating stories of the great discoverers and their discoveries. All the authors have been selected both for expertness in the fields they discuss and for ability to communicate their special knowledge and their own views in an interesting way. The primary purpose of these books is to provide a survey of physics within the grasp of the young student or the layman. Many of the books, it is hoped, will encourage the reader to make his own investigations of natural phenomena.

The Series, which now offers topics on all the sciences and their applications, had its beginning in a project to revise the secondary schools' physics curriculum. At the Massachusetts Institute of Technology during 1956 a group of physicists, high school teachers, journalists, apparatus designers, film producers, and other specialists organized the Physical Science Study Committee, now operating as a part of Educational Services Incorporated, Watertown, Massachusetts. They pooled their knowledge and experience toward the design and creation of aids to the learning of physics. Initially their effort was supported by the National Science Foundation, which has continued to aid the program. The Ford Foundation, the Fund for the Advancement of Education, and the Alfred P. Sloan Foundation have also given support. The Committee has created a textbook, an extensive film series, a laboratory guide, especially designed apparatus, and a teacher's source book.

The Series is guided by a Board of Editors, consisting of Bruce F. Kingsbury, Managing Editor; John H. Durston, General Editor; Paul F. Brandwein, the Conservation Foundation and Harcourt, Brace & World, Inc.; Francis L. Friedman, Massachusetts Institute of Technology; Samuel A. Goudsmit, Brookhaven National Laboratory; Philippe LeCorbeiller, Harvard University; and Herbert S. Zim, Simon and Schuster, Inc.

# PREFACE

This book appeared originally as a series of articles in *The Illustrated London News,* a British weekly picture magazine of immense respectability, which devotes considerable space to adroit and authoritative writing on science. The author is a distinguished mathematician, physicist and cosmologist, best known as one of the three principal proponents of the steady-state theory of the expanding universe. As you will learn in the pages that follow, there are today two main (and mutually exclusive) schools of thought on the origin and operation of the physical universe; the steady-state theory is one of them. The Board of Editors has chosen Professor Bondi's articles for the Science Study Series not only because any book in layman's terms from the typewriter of an outstanding scientist is a rare prize to be seized forthwith, but also because Professor Bondi's writing has the rarely attained virtue of simplicity. As he guides you on this tour of the universe, he explains the sights in words you can understand.

The English Professor Bondi writes so pleasantly is not his native language (a situation that seems to occur more often in our literature than in others). He was born, on November 1, 1919, in Vienna, Austria, and received his elementary and secondary schooling there. His father was a physician and his sister became one, but Hermann early turned a deaf ear to the family vocation, too worrying a business. At the *Realgymnasium,*

9

counterpart of our high school, he was enough interested in mathematics and theoretical physics to plow into some moderately advanced textbooks on his own. In 1937 he entered Trinity College, Cambridge, England, to read mathematics. On the strength of his performance there he became an Exhibitioner after one year and a Senior Scholar after two.

When World War II got under way in earnest, the British interned Bondi as an Austrian subject and sent him to Canada. (His family meanwhile had escaped from Austria just ahead of Hitler and made their way to New York, where his father practiced medicine until his death in 1959.) Bondi stayed in Canada until the summer of 1941 and then returned to Cambridge, which in his absence had given him the B.A. degree. After some research on hydrodynamics he joined a secret Admiralty project on radar and there met Fred Hoyle, the astrophysicist, who aroused Bondi's interest in astronomy and cosmology. Together, and occasionally on His Majesty's office time, they managed to do a substantial piece of work on the interaction of interstellar gas and stars. For his share in this work, Bondi was made a Fellow of Trinity College in 1943. It was at this same Admiralty project that he, Hoyle and Thomas Gold began the intellectual collaboration that has made them the big three of the steady-state theory.

When Bondi assumed his Trinity Fellowship in 1945, he received appointment to an assistant lectureship at Cambridge University. Despite the demands of the classroom, the research laboratory and the bridge table, he found time to collaborate with Hoyle on problems in mathematical physics and with Raymond Arthur Lyttleton in astronomical work. In 1947 he and Christine Mary Stockman, a research student of Hoyle's, were married, and they subsequently published a series of joint papers on stellar structure. The Bondis have three daughters and two sons.

The Bondi home in Cambridge became a meeting place for Hoyle, Gold and other colleagues, and long conversations on the structure of the universe bore fruit in 1948 in a Bondi and Gold paper setting forth the steady-state theory. Not long afterward Hoyle published a paper that arrived at much the same conclusions by a very different route.

Bondi left Cambridge in 1954 and became Professor of Applied Mathematics at King's College, University of London. He has spent a term at Cornell University (1951) as a research associate and had a similar post at the Harvard College Observatory (1953). In the latter year he delivered the Lowell Lectures in Boston. He is a Fellow of the Royal Astronomical Society, and its secretary since 1956, a Fellow of the Royal Society and a Fellow of the Cambridge Philosophical Society. In addition to the numerous technical papers he has published, he is the author of *Cosmology* (Cambridge University Press, 1952), which at this writing he was revising to incorporate late developments. In recent years he has concentrated on gravitational theory and general relativity and made contributions to the problems of negative mass and gravitational waves. Bondi describes himself as a "lazy reader" who prefers to hear about his colleagues' work by word of mouth instead of through the technical journals. This preference for casual but effective communication of scientific ideas perhaps has contributed to the easy style of *The Universe at Large*.

JOHN H. DURSTON

# CONTENTS

The Science Study Series                                      7

Preface                                                      9

I. The Expansion of the Universe                            17
*The Methods of Science—Expansion of
the Universe—The Red Shift—Velocity
of Receding Stars*

II. Why Is It Dark at Night?                                27
*Olbers' Paradox—The Mathematics of
Starlight—Expansion and Dimness*

III. Theories of Cosmology                                  35
*Relativistic Cosmologies: An Evolv-
ing Universe—Lemaître's Explosion—
Steady-State Cosmologies—How Continuous Creation Works*

IV. Tests in Cosmology                                      47
*The Ages of Galaxies—The Evolution of
Galaxies—Origin of the Elements*

V. The Stars                                                57
*Distances of the Stars: Parallax—Color
and Temperature—Size and Mass of
Stars*

VI. What Goes on inside the Stars                           67
*Red Giants, White Dwarfs and the
Main Sequence—The Structure of Stars*

*—Answering Eddington's Question—The*
*Burning of Hydrogen*

VII.   Between the Stars   79
*Cosmic Haze—Polarization of Light—*
*Polarized Starlight—Electrical Currents*
*in Space*

VIII.   The Earth's Radiation Belts   89
*The Aurora—Trapped Particles—Mag-*
*netic Bottles—Magnetism in Space*

IX.   The Law of Gravitation   99
*Inverse Square Law—Tunnels through*
*the Earth—Weightlessness—Einstein's*
*Gravity*

X.   The Motion of Celestial Bodies   111
*The Sun's Force—The Orbits of Satel-*
*lites—The Speed of Meteors—Gravity*
*and Light*

XI.   The Tides   121
*Forces between Double Stars—Sun Tides*
*vs. Moon Tides—The Reason for Higher*
*Tides—Tidal Friction—Atmospheric*
*Tides—Tidal Resonance*

XII.   The Earth: Motion and Magnetism   133
*Wobble of the Earth's Axis—Shift of the*
*Earth's Axis—Source of the Earth's Mag-*
*netism*

Index   143

# THE UNIVERSE AT LARGE

# I. The Expansion of the Universe

The conventional manner of describing the astronomer's universe is to start at the earth and work outward. In these essays we are going to start at the most distant objects observed and work our way inward. There is something to be said for this method of procedure. It is true that we start with what is most unfamiliar, the objects about which least is known. But then, we always have a hankering suspicion that it is when we go to the very, very large, or to the very, very small, that we shall find simplicity. This is not unreasonable. For we know that we, ourselves, are among the most complex things that nature produces, and the enormous complexity of the higher living animals seems to correspond to a size far larger than the atomic scale and far smaller than the astronomer's scale. Perhaps this enormous complexity, of which we are just an example, is associated with size, and both in the very, very small and in the enormously large, nature is rather simpler than at our own medium scale.

Of course, one can also take a different attitude. One can say that it is the natural progress of science to start with very little knowledge, to form theories based on this knowledge, then to make further observations that complicate the picture, and so on, until eventually a very complex situation is reached. When we consider the very, very large, then so little is known that we have got only rather few items of information to put into our theories. This does not mean that they are bad theories.

17

We try to make our present theories the best that one can have at the present state of knowledge. It is never any good in science to cry for the fullest information. We have never got it. One always has to do with what we have and make the best of the job in hand at the moment.

## The Methods of Science

This may be a good moment to discuss the methods of science. To the outsider, science often seems to be a frightful jumble of facts with very little that looks human and inspiring about it. To the working scientist, it is so full of interest and so fascinating that he can only pity the layman. The imaginative character of science is more apparent in some branches than in others. But there are many features that are common to the whole range of scientific work, and these are the methods of science. Where an activity is going on at the speed and with the pressure with which scientific work is pursued, it is often difficult to pause and analyze just what one is actually doing. Fortunately, this has been done for us by the philosophers of science, and by none with more insight and understanding and accuracy than by Karl Popper, whose book on the subject, published over twenty years ago, has recently appeared in an English translation.* His analysis is so profound and rings so true that it may be useful to describe it here in brief. The essential point that Popper makes with such force is that the real basis of science is the possibility of empirical disproof. It is not proof that is of importance in science; on the contrary, he claims, proof can never be given.

* Popper, Karl R., *Logic of Scientific Discovery,* Basic Books, 1959.

We can, however, say that certain statements are definitely incorrect. We can *disprove* them.

In his picture, the scientist formulates a theory, inspired, of course, by the existing knowledge. He then uses this theory to make forecasts of what new experiments should reveal; of what the results of fresh observations ought to be, according to his theory. If, then, these experiments are carried out and disagree with the prognostications of the theory, we know that the theory is wrong. If, on the other hand, the experiments agree with the theory, then it is the task of the theory to forecast more and more new experiments so that it can be tested and tested again and so on. None of these tests can prove a theory, but any one of them is capable of disproving it. For even if, up to a certain point, all the experiments agree with the forecast of the theory, yet new ones may come along in the future that may show it to have been wrong after all. This, indeed, seems to be the fate of many scientific theories, however successful they may have been for a long time. The most famous example is Newton's Law of Gravitation, on the basis of which the astronomers predicted the positions of the planets and the moon and the eclipses and all the many phenomena of the solar system successfully for well over two hundred years. Then a new theory of gravitation came along, Einstein's theory. It turned out that the predictions of Einstein's theory were almost identical with those of Newton's theory, and so all the many tests that have been in accord with the forecasts of Newton's theory were in agreement with the forecasts of Einstein's theory. However, in one or two small details there turned out to be a slight difference between the theories. These observations are in favor of Einstein's and against Newton's theory. Hence, in spite of the enormous number of cases where Newton's theory has been correct, it is no longer regarded as true in any sense; but we know from its close agreement with Einstein's theory that, except for a few very small details, Newton's theory will give the same answers as Einstein's. As Newton's theory is much simpler mathematically, we go on using it as a useful tool of astronomical work, not as something we believe to be true in any sense of the word.

In cosmology, as the science of the universe at large is called, one must be particularly careful to adhere to the rules of scientific work. For so little is known, and the subject appeals to us so much and excites our imaginations to such an extent that, unless we are very careful, we might allow it to run away with us. The procedure that we must follow is the same as in all science: we must formulate theories with a view to their forecasts being tested by observation. The more forecasts a theory can make, the more they are accessible to observational disproof; the more testable the theory is, the better it is. However much the picture drawn by a theory may appeal to us, the purpose of the theory is to suggest observations by means of which it might be disproved. It is with this in view that we must consider the evidence we have on the universe.

### Expansion of the Universe

The most striking feature of the universe is probably its expansion. What exactly is the evidence for this and how strong is it? In Plate I we have a picture that displays some of the evidence in striking form. A series of pictures of galaxies is shown in the left-hand column. They are all taken with the same telescope, using the same magnification. On the right-hand side we see the spectra of these galaxies. Now, first, what is a spectrum? It is well known that white light is a combination of all the colors and that it can be broken up into these colors by suitable aids; a rainbow is a familiar instance. A handier means is the use of a prism of glass or other suitable material; with its aid the whole band of colors of sunlight is spread out. If one uses a prism that spreads out the sunlight very clearly, then one notices that the colors do not form a smooth band and that in numerous places dark lines run across the spectrum. The origin of these lines is rather complicated. In the main they are due to the light from the sun shining through cooler gases of the sun's atmosphere, and these gases happen to be opaque to very particular colors, to thin lines, and so leave a part of the spectrum dark. The astronomer can use spectroscopes of great power to analyze the light of individual stars and also of individual galaxies. Naturally, particularly for the very distant galaxies, rather little light is available, and because of that, and for more technical reasons, the spectrum of a galaxy will not be nearly as clear as, say, the spectrum of the sun. Nevertheless, a few of the very prominent dark lines do show up, even in the spectra of these distant galaxies. The remarkable phenomenon that was discovered nearly forty years ago is that these lines are not where they ought to be, not where they are in the case of the sun, say, but they are displaced; they are shifted. The shift is always toward the red and is indicated in the illustrations of the spectra in Plate I. You will notice that the fainter and smaller the galaxy looks, the greater the shift of the spectrum toward the red. This is a full description of the direct observational result. A red shift of the spectrum is observed and is correlated with the apparent brightness of the galaxy, so that the fainter the galaxy, the greater the red shift. From here on we start on a series of interpretations.

## The Red Shift

First, what can be the explanation of such a red shift? In what other circumstances are red shifts observed? The answer is that, but for one rather insignificant cause, the red shift always indicates a velocity of recession. Unfamiliar as the phenomenon is in the case of light, it is commonly noticed in the case of sound. If a whistling railway train speeds past you, then you notice that, to your ears, the pitch of the whistle drops markedly as the train passes you. The reason for this is not difficult to understand. The whistle produces sound; sound is a vibration of the air in which pressure maxima and pressure minima succeed each other periodically; these travel toward your ears where they are turned into nerve impulses that enter your consciousness. While the train is approaching, each successive pressure maximum has a smaller distance to travel to reach you. Therefore, the time interval between the reception of the pressure maxima will be less than the time interval between their emission. We say that the pitch of the note is raised. Conversely, when the train is receding from you, each successive pressure maximum has farther to travel and, therefore, the pressure maxima will reach your ear at intervals of time greater than the intervals at which they were emitted. Accordingly, the pitch is lower. How great the raising or the lowering of the pitch is, depends on the ratio of the velocity of the train to the velocity of sound, which is about 1100 ft. per second.

Very much the same thing happens with light, but

here an increase in the pitch becomes noticed as a shift toward the violet; a decrease in the pitch becomes noticed as a shift toward the red. Also, the crucial velocity is now not that of sound, but the very much higher velocity of light at 186,000 miles per second. A red shift, therefore, indicates a velocity of recession of the source; a velocity standing to the velocity of light in the ratio given by the magnitude of the red shift—that is, by the change in wave length divided by the wave length. The velocities so derived from the observed red shifts are shown on the right-hand side of Plate I. Such a velocity of recession is, then, the only cause of the red shift that we can infer from our terrestrial knowledge of physics. What about the other characteristic of the picture, this time the characteristic of the photographs on the left, the increasing faintness and diminishing size? We all know that an object of a given brightness will look fainter the farther away it is. There is very little else in astronomy to guide us about the distances of these galaxies which we see so very far away. Accordingly, if we interpret the faintness of the galaxies as indicators of their distances, and the red shift of the spectra as velocities of recession, then we find that the velocity of recession is proportional to the distance of the object.

## Velocity of Receding Stars

We have inferred a "velocity-distance law" from the red shift-brightness relation. For a long time physicists and astronomers felt rather uneasy about these enormous velocities of recession that seemed to follow from their observations. They argued that all our interpretation was based on our local knowledge of physics, and that unknown effects might well occur in the depth of the universe that somehow falsify the picture that we receive. Nowadays, we have little patience with this type of argument. For the expansion of the universe is not merely given by the observation of the spectrum. We have also noted the remarkable uniformity of the universe, how it looks the same in all directions around us if only we look sufficiently far. If, then, we suppose that the universe is, indeed, uniform on a very large scale, we can ask the mathematical question: How can it move and yet maintain its uniformity? The answer is that it can only move in such a way that the velocity of every object is in the line of sight and proportional to its distance. This is the only type of motion that will maintain uniformity. Therefore, we are again driven to the conclusion that an expansion with a velocity of recession proportional to distance is a natural consequence of the assumption of uniformity which is also based on observation. Furthermore, if we try to form a theory of the universe, whichever way we do it, we always come up with the answer that it is almost bound to be in motion, with objects showing velocities proportional to their distances.

I must again stress the uniformity of the system. We are not in a privileged position on the basis of these assumptions, but in a typical one. The universe would present the same appearance to observers on any other galaxy. They would see the same effects; the same red shift-brightness relation. Though no one can be certain of anything in this field, we do see that there are different lines of argument all converging to the conclusion that the red shifts should indeed be taken as indicating velocities of recession proportional to the distance of the objects. If we divide the distance of any galaxy by its velocity of recession, we get the same number whatever galaxy we choose. That follows from the proportionality of velocity and distance. This number is a time, a time that, according to the most recent work, is about 10,000 million years. In some way or other this is the characteristic time of the universe.

THE UNIVERSE AT LARGE

without considering any of the phenomena discovered by modern astronomy.

Olbers then attempted to calculate what the bright-

## II. Why Is It Dark at Night?

One of the bases of modern cosmology is known as Olbers' paradox, which makes the darkness of the night sky appear as a curious phenomenon. The argument leading up to this is so simple and attractive and beautiful that it may not be out of place to consider it here in full.

When one looks at the sky at night one notices that there are some very bright stars, more medium bright ones and very large numbers of faint ones. It is easy to see that this phenomenon might be accounted for by the fact that the bright-looking stars happen to be near; the medium bright ones rather farther away, and the faint ones a good deal farther away still. In this way one would not only account for the variations in brightness but also for the fact that there are more of the faint ones than of the medium bright ones, and more of the medium bright ones than of the very bright ones, for there is more space farther away than nearby. One can now speculate about stars yet farther away, so far away, in fact, that they cannot be seen individually, not by the naked eye, nor even by the telescope. The question then arises of whether these very distant stars, though they would individually be too faint to be seen, might not be so exceedingly numerous as to provide an even background illumination of the night sky? This is the question that the German astronomer Olbers asked 130-odd years ago. The argument will now be presented in the light of the astronomical knowledge of 1826, without considering any of the phenomena discovered by modern astronomy.

## Olbers' Paradox

Olbers then attempted to calculate what the brightness of the background of the sky should be on this basis. He immediately realized that in trying to consider effects from regions too far away to be seen in detail, he was forced to make assumptions about what the depths of the universe were like. He then made a set of assumptions which looks so plausible even nowadays that they may well serve as a model of what the beginning of a scientific investigation should be like. He first assumed, in the light of the knowledge of his day (1826), that the distant regions of the universe would be very much like our own. He expected there would be stars there, with the same average distance between them as between near stars. He expected that while each star would have an intrinsic brightness of its own, there would be an average brightness of stars very much like that in our astronomical neighborhood. In other words, he assumed that we get a typical view of the universe. This is in full accord with the ideas that have been current since the days of Copernicus, that there is nothing special, nothing pre-selected about our position in the scheme of things. This is a convenient assumption from a scientific point of view and a very fruitful one because we can assume that what goes on around us holds elsewhere as well, if not in detail at least on the average.

Unfortunately, this assumption is not sufficient for the calculation Olbers wished to make. For light travels at a finite speed: at a high speed, it is true, but a finite one nevertheless. The light we now receive from many distant regions was sent out by the objects there a long time ago, having spent the intervening period on its journey from there to here. What is important for us, therefore, in trying to calculate the amount of light we get from the depths of the universe, is not how much the stars there radiate *now,* but how much they radiated at the time when the light which we receive now was sent out by them. We have to make a guess about the variation of astronomical conditions, not only with space, but also with time. And here, again, Olbers made the simplest of all possible assumptions, for he assumed time to matter as little as space. In other words, he supposed that not only in other parts of the universe, but also at other times, there would be stars, that their brightness would be the same as it is in our astronomical neighborhood, and similarly, their average distance apart would be the same as it is near us. Next, Olbers assumed, very naturally, that the laws of physics, as we know them from here, apply elsewhere and at other times. In particular, he assumed that the laws of the propagation of light— the way light spreads out after leaving its source—applied over these vast regions just as much as they apply in our rooms here. This, again, is the most obvious, most convenient and most fruitful assumption one can make. It would seem a stupid thing to set out on a voyage of discovery into the depths of the universe by first throwing away all the knowledge we have gained in our vicinity. Finally, Olbers made an assumption which is of the utmost importance, but he made it implicitly. He was not aware of the fact that he was making an assumption at all. Scientists know very well that this is the most dangerous kind of assumption. This assumption was that there were no large, systematic motions in the universe; that the universe was static.

## The Mathematics of Starlight

On the basis of these four assumptions, it is easy to work out the background light of the sky. Imagine a vast, spherical shell surrounding us. (See Fig. 1.) The

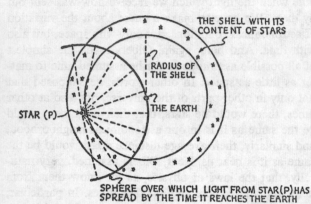

FIG. 1. *Each star gives off a large amount of light but only a small fraction reaches our earth. But there are so many millions of stars a large amount of light should reach us. If we consider shells of equal thickness, equal amounts of light should reach us from each shell. If this were so, the sky should be bright and there would be neither night nor day nor any life on earth.*

thickness of the shell is supposed to be small compared with its radius; but the whole shell is supposed to be so enormous that there are vast numbers of stars within the shell. How many stars are there in this shell? In order to work this out we have to know the volume of the shell. If we call the radius of the shell $R$ and its thickness $H$, then we see readily that the surface of the sphere on which the shell is built is $4\pi R^2$ and thus the volume of the shell is, to a sufficient approximation, $4\pi R^2 H$. If, now, $N$ is the number of stars per unit volume, then the number of stars in the shell of volume $4\pi R^2 H$ will be $4\pi R^2 HN$. How much light will all the stars in the shell send out? If the average rate at which an individual star sends out light is $L$, then all the stars in the shell put together will send out $4\pi R^2 HNL$. However, what interests us is not how much light all these stars send out, but how much light we receive from them. Consider the light of an individual star in the shell. By the time the light from it reaches us, it will have traveled through a distance $R$: and so it will have spread out over a sphere of surface $4\pi R^2$. That is to say, the light of each individual star has to be divided by $4\pi R^2$ to tell us the intensity of light from it which is received here. This is true of all the stars in the shell, and, therefore, the total light we receive from all the stars in the shell is the total light they send out divided by $4\pi R^2$. This division leads to the cancellation of the factor $4\pi R^2$ and we are left with $HNL$.

It will be seen that this does not involve the radius of the shell at all. The amount of light we receive from any shell of equal thickness is the same irrespective of the radius of the shell. If, therefore, we add shell after shell, then, since we get the same amount of light from each shell, the amount received will go up and up without limit. On this basis, we should be receiving an infinite amount of light from all the shells stretching out to infinity. However, this argument not only leads to an absurd conclusion, but is not quite right. For each star, in addition to sending out light, obstructs the light from the stars beyond it. In other words, we will not be receiving light from stars in the very distant shells because

there will generally be a star in between us and there—
a nearer star—which will intercept the light. Of course,
it will be realized that stars send out very much light,
considering how small a surface they have. Therefore,
this obscuring or shadowing effect is not very strong; it
will prevent the sum from going up to infinity, but it
still leads to our getting from all these shells of stars a
flood of light equal to 50,000 times sunlight when the
sun is in the zenith. On this basis, then, it should be in-
credibly bright both day and night. Everything would
be burned up; it would correspond to a temperature of
over 10,000 degrees Fahrenheit. Naturally, this remarkable result astonished Olbers, and he tried to find a way
out. He thought that this flood of light might be stopped
by obscuring clouds of matter in space between us and
these distant stars. However, this way of escape does not
work. For, if there were such a cloud, it would be getting hot owing to the very fact that it was absorbing
light from stars; and it would go on getting hotter and
hotter until it radiated by its glow as much light as it
received from the stars. And then it would not be a
shield worth having any longer. Other ways out have
been tried, but none of them works. We are, therefore,
inevitably led to the result that, on the basis of Olbers'
assumptions, we should be receiving a flood of light
which is not, in fact, observed.

## Expansion and Dimness

This little argument may well serve as a prototype of
scientific arguments. We start with a theory, the set of
assumptions that Olbers made. We have deduced from
them by a logical argument consequences that are sus-
ceptible to observation, namely, the brightness of the

sky. We have found that the forecasts of the theory do not agree with observation, and thus the assumptions on which the theory is based must be wrong. We know, as a result of Olbers' work, that whatever may be going on in the depths of the universe, they cannot be constructed in accordance with his assumptions. By this method of empirical disproof, we have discovered something about the universe and so have made cosmology a science.

In order to escape from this paradox, we have to drop at least one of his assumptions. In the light of modern knowledge described in the previous chapter, the reader will have no difficulty in spotting the assumption that has to be dropped. It is the one that the universe is static. If the universe is expanding, then the distant stars will be moving away from us at highest speeds, and, it is well known from ordinary physics that light emitted by a receding source is reduced in intensity compared with light emitted by a source at rest. With an expanding universe, such as the one we live in, it may indeed be dark at night, for the light from the distant shells is tremendously weakened by the fact that the luminous objects in them are rushing away from us at high speed. Thus, the darkness of the night sky, the most obvious of all astronomical observations, leads us almost directly to the expansion of the universe, this remarkable and outstanding phenomenon discovered by modern astronomy.

Other changes made by modern astronomy in Olbers' assumptions are relatively minor. It is true that we know that our stars do not go on and on, but form a large stellar system, our galaxy; but we also know that beyond our galaxy there are millions and millions of other galaxies, all more or less like ours. We could, therefore, put

Olbers' argument into modern language by changing the reference to stars going on and on in space to galaxies going on and on. The substance of the argument would not be affected. Not only are the galaxies individually remarkable objects (they fall into various types), but they appear to be most extraordinarily sociable. Very few, if any, of them occur singly in space. Most of them stick together to form clusters of galaxies. Some of these clusters do not contain a very large number of members, like our own local cluster of galaxies; but some of them are extraordinarily rich and contain vast numbers. Some, indeed, are supposed to contain 10,000 or more individual galaxies. It is one of the major tasks of the theory of cosmology not only to account for the existence of the galaxies themselves, but even more to account for the remarkable fact that they form these vast clusters.

# III. Theories of Cosmology

In the previous chapter a number of the remarkable features of the universe have been mentioned: the galaxies; the uniformity of their distribution over the sky; the darkness of the night sky; the expansion of the universe; the clustering of the galaxies. Just as in other fields of science, one asks in cosmology, too, for a theory that will link and correlate the observations mentioned and others which are of a more recondite nature. Here, as elsewhere in science, it is, however, the chief task of a theory to forecast the results of new observations; to suggest methods of shooting down the theory. In this way, theories inspire new observations, and it is this method that exposes as foolish the suggestion that it is too early to formulate theories of cosmology; that we should wait until further information has been gathered before forming theories. We can never wait until we have all the facts at our disposal; that time never comes. We must always try to do the best with what we have got. Of course, we would be foolish to regard our present theories as infallible or final. It is not the purpose of any scientific theory ever to be infallible or final or true. Its purpose is to be fertile; to suggest new observations that suggest new ramifications of the subject.

In a subject in which so little information is available as in cosmology, it need not, therefore, come as a surprise that there are several different theories in the field. They all account more or less well for the existing observations, but they differ sharply in their forecasts of future ones. Two of these theories have received particularly great attention. Their consequences have been worked out in some detail, and they will be described here in brief.

## Relativistic Cosmologies: An Evolving Universe

The first theory or, rather, class of theories, is known as relativistic cosmology. The basis of this class of theory is the general theory of relativity proposed by Albert Einstein forty-five years ago. This is the best theory of gravitation we have. It agrees with all the enormous multitude of observations on the effects of gravitation in the solar system. Relativistic cosmology is essentially an attempt to apply this highly successful theory of gravitation to the universe at large. For this purpose another assumption has to be added to it, and this is the assumption of the large-scale uniformity of the universe. As has been said previously, there is a good deal of astronomical evidence in favor of such an assumption. Many models of the universe can be constructed on this basis. However, some of them appear to be much more promising as representations of our actual universe than others; and foremost among these is the model due to the Belgian Abbé Lemaître. This model shares with all other models of relativistic cosmology the property of being evolving, that is, of the universe as a whole undergoing changes in the course of time.

Any model in which the universe as a whole undergoes changes is described as an evolutionary model. All models of relativistic cosmology are evolutionary models. In Lemaître's model the universe is finite, but unbounded. Though, at first sight, this seems an odd concept, there is nothing queer about it. It is purely a matter of local experience that if I move away from a point in a straight line I get farther and farther away from it all the time. To suggest that this remains correct however far I go is nothing but an assumption, an extrapolation from locally gained knowledge. A finite universe is simply one where, if I go on and on and on, eventually (admittedly after a very, very long walk) I get back to the place where I started from. In two dimensions this is familiar from the case of the earth. If I keep on going in the same direction, eventually I will come back to where I started from, having encircled the earth. It is true that the surface of the earth is a two-dimensional surface, but the suggestion is that the same situation should apply on an enormously larger scale in the universe in three dimensions. Strange and unfamiliar as this concept may sound, there is no reason to be surprised that, when we talk about distances of thousands of millions of light-years, we should be encountering a strange and unusual experience.

## Lemaître's Explosion

Though the total volume of the universe is now vast, in Lemaître's model it was fairly small to start with. This, of course, was very long ago—possibly 40 thousand million years ago. The same amount of matter that now fills the universe so thinly was then confined to a comparatively small space and, accordingly, was very dense and also very hot. Some sort of nuclear explosion occurred so that the entire model started by expanding rapidly. However, owing to the great density of matter, the force of gravitation was strong, and so the expansion was slowed down by the force of gravitation. In general relativity, in addition to the usual force of gravitation,

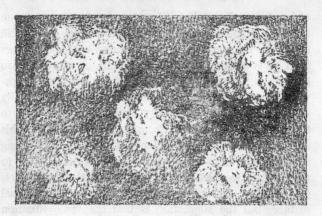

FIG. 2. *In the young universe, according to Lemaître, the hot dense gas is rapidly expanding in the entire universe.*

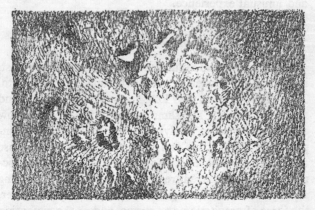

FIG. 3. *In the adolescent universe, according to Lemaître, the gas has cooled and in a vast cloud, like a fog, is now almost at rest.*

FIG. 4. *In the middle-aged universe, according to Le-maître, the gas has cooled further after the passing of thousands of millions of years and eventually forms into galaxies.*

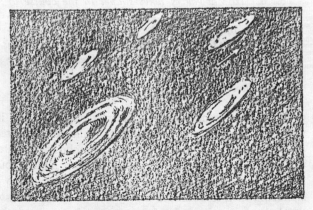

FIG. 5. *In the old universe, according to Lemaître, the galaxies conform to the expansion of the universe and rush away from each other.*

there may also be a universal force of repulsion increasing with distance. As long as the model was small, as long as matter was dense, gravitation was much more powerful than this long-range force of repulsion. How-

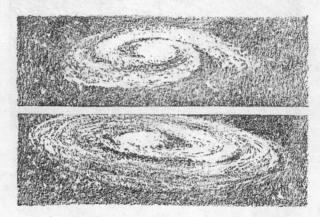

FIG. 6. *How a galaxy takes shape: In the course of time the shapeless cloud of gas by contraction commences to rotate (top) and as the speed of rotation increases the gas forms into a flat disc with a glowing bulge in the center (bottom). The diameter may be about 100,000 light-years or six hundred thousand million million miles.*

ever, as the system expanded, it approached a state in which the force of gravitation exactly balanced the force of repulsion. By the time the system reached this state, the motion of expansion had slowed down almost, but not entirely, to a standstill. Had the universe got to a standstill, then it would have stayed as it was, owing to the balance between the force of gravitation and the force of repulsion. As, however, it was still expanding, though very, very slowly, it remained in more or less

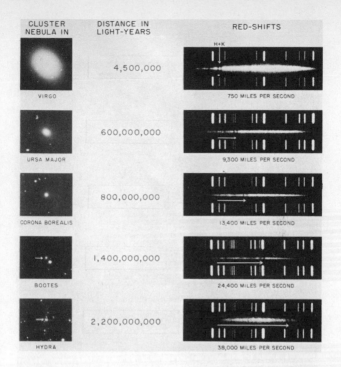

| CLUSTER NEBULA IN | DISTANCE IN LIGHT-YEARS | RED-SHIFTS |
|---|---|---|
| VIRGO | 4,500,000 | H+K ... 750 MILES PER SECOND |
| URSA MAJOR | 600,000,000 | 9,300 MILES PER SECOND |
| CORONA BOREALIS | 800,000,000 | 13,400 MILES PER SECOND |
| BOOTES | 1,400,000,000 | 24,400 MILES PER SECOND |
| HYDRA | 2,200,000,000 | 38,000 MILES PER SECOND |

PLATE I. *The expansion of the universe is inferred from these and similar observations. The left-hand column shows galaxies at various distances photographed with the same magnification. In each photograph the galaxy appears as a diffuse object with its center in the middle of the picture, but the two most distant ones are marked by arrows for purposes of identification. The other diffuse objects in the photographs are other galaxies, the sharp ones being stars near to us. On the right are photographs of the diffuse-looking spectra of the galaxies stretching in each case from blue on the left to red on the right. The bright lines above and below each spectrum are produced in the laboratory and serve only as markers. The pair of dark lines in the spectrum of each galaxy above the tip of the arrow would be above the foot of the arrow if the source were at rest.*

**PLATE II.** *A view of the famous Mount Palomar Observatory, California, showing the dome of the huge 200-inch telescope.*

PLATE III.    *Looking down the 200-inch Hale telescope at Mount Palomar, from outside the dome. The observer is in the cage at the focus of the great circular mirror lower down.*

PLATE IV. *A photograph of a cluster of galaxies in* Coma Berenices *at a distance of about 200 million light-years. Most galaxies occur in such clusters.*

this state of balance for a fair length of time; but then, having expanded just a little beyond this equilibrium, the force of repulsion turned out to be stronger than gravitation. Hence expansion continued and accelerated; the expansion became faster and will go on for all time. We are now, according to the theory, in this second phase of expansion of the universe.

In the first phase of expansion the initially very hot gas cooled down gradually; the long, intermediate state, when the universe was almost, though not quite, at a standstill, is supposed to have been the time when the gas, now fairly cool, condensed into clusters of galaxies and these again into individual galaxies. At that stage, then, the density of matter was just right for the formation of galaxies. Now, when, owing to the renewed expansion, the density is very much lower, no new galaxies can be formed. This model of the universe, therefore, has many different phases. A youthful, exuberant phase of high temperature and expansion; a middle period of condensation into galaxies in a situation of almost complete rest; and an old age in which the galaxies, themselves aging, are rushing away from each other in a renewed process of expansion, continually depleting the density of the universe still further. We are now in this late stage; or, as Lemaître himself has put it, of the fireworks that started the universe only a few hot ashes are left, and these are our galaxies.

## Steady-State Cosmologies

In complete contrast to the evolutionary models of relativistic cosmology (of which Lemaître's is only one) stands the steady-state theory. The basis of this theory, as its name implies, is the assumption that the universe is not only uniform in space, but also unchanging in time when viewed on a sufficiently large scale. This seems to be the simplest possible model of the universe and the one in which our locally gained knowledge of physics can be applied with the greatest amount of confidence. For all our science has been learned in—cosmologically speaking—a minute region in a very short period of time. Unless ours is a typical place and time, we cannot have much confidence in the applicability of our science elsewhere in the universe and at other times. Of course, this assumption of uniformity in space and time does not mean that the universe must conform to it. It only means that this seems a very good model to investigate because, owing to the confidence with which one can apply one's knowledge to all sorts of problems in it, one can make more and better forecasts by means of which the theory is open to the check of observation.

The most remarkable feature of this theory is the process of continual creation. Owing to the expansion of the universe, the mean density of matter would appear to be diminishing all the time, contrary to the assumption that the system is unchanging. If we wish to remain true to our assumptions, therefore, we have no choice but to postulate that there is going on everywhere and at all times a continual creation of matter, the appearance of atoms of hydrogen out of nothing. The rate of this continual creation is very low indeed, owing to the tenuous distribution of matter in the universe and the slowness of the expansion, as measured by terrestrial standards. In the whole of the volume of the earth it would amount only to a mass like that of a particle of dust every million years or so. Clearly, this is far below anything that could be measured directly and does not contradict the experiments or the experiences on which the usual law of conservation of matter is based. On the other hand, there is no doubt that it seems strange to us. Naturally, if we stray far from our usual environment where our experiences have been formed, we must not be surprised to find something strange. The mathematicians, too, find continuous creation inconvenient, having worked for a long time with a mathematically absolute law of conservation of matter. However, mathematical convenience is not a good guide in scientific progress.

## How Continuous Creation Works

What, then, does this steady-state universe look like? Although it is unchanging on a large scale, it is not unchanging in detail. Each individual galaxy ages owing to the way its resources of hydrogen are being depleted by its conversion into helium inside the stars, and for other reasons. However, the aging of the individual members of the universe does not imply that the universe as a whole is aging. If we look at a human population, then each individual is born, grows up, grows old and dies; but if we look at the population in a statistical way, then no change seems to take place, at least if our population is stationary, which is the case we shall consider. Then, the number of children ten years old will be the same at one time as it is at any other, although, of course, the individuals will be different. Similarly, the fraction of the population over the age of sixty-five will be the same at all times, though, again, it will be composed of different individuals. Hence, a bird's-eye view of the system will always be the same. This is just like the universe of the steady-state theory. Individual galaxies age and move apart from each other owing to the expansion. In the increasing spaces between them, newly

FIG. 7. *To visualize the steady-state theory, think of an epoch when a certain region of space contains seven galaxies receding from each other.*

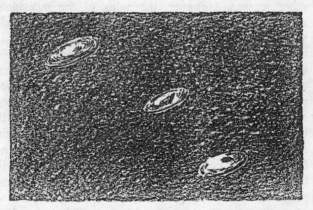

FIG. 8. *If no new galaxy were formed, the region of space of Fig. 7 would look like this. Recession of the original galaxies would leave the region "depopulated" as the universe expanded.*

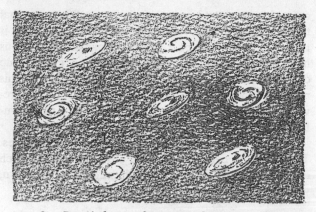

FIG. 9.    *But if the steady-state explanation is the correct one, new galaxies would form and take the place of the older galaxies that moved away. Again the region of space would contain seven galaxies, as in Fig. 7.*

FIG. 10.    *In the progression from the situation of Fig. 7 through Fig. 9 there is, if the steady-state theory prevails, a continuous passing away into space of older galaxies, and new galaxies condensed out of newly created matter take their places.*

created matter condenses to form new galaxies, so that the average distance remains the same. Condensation is the process of birth of a galaxy; expansion to regions hard to see is the process of death, and growing up comes in between. Although each galaxy ages in this manner, a bird's-eye view of the system will always reveal the same picture, just as in the case of our population.

This completes our description of the two theories. The tests that can be made, the observations by which one or the other, or possibly both, might be shot down, will form the subject of the next chapter.

# IV. Tests in Cosmology

In the last chapter attention was drawn to the difference between the evolutionary models in which the universe as a whole undergoes changes in the course of time, and the steady-state model in which the universe always presents the same appearance at all times when viewed on a sufficiently large scale. The purpose of these theories is to suggest observations by means of which their forecasts can be checked. Of course, not all the detailed statements of the theory can be available for test. For example, the exceedingly low rate of continual creation required by the steady-state theory is not directly accessible to tests. But if the consequences of the theory can be tested and are found to agree with observation, then we would feel much more inclined to accept on this indirect evidence the idea of continual creation.

In cosmology there is, fortunately, a considerable number of possible tests that could discriminate between the most important theories of the present day, tests that can be performed with existing observing equipment, though they may well be near the limit of what this equipment can do. Some of these tests will now be described in detail.

## The Ages of Galaxies

If we look at distant regions of the universe, we do not see them as they are now, but we see them as they were when the light that we receive now was sent out.

Though the velocity of light is large, the distances are so enormous that the light takes a long time to get here. In the case of some objects we can see, the light has probably taken several billion years to get here. Accordingly, we see these objects not as they are now, but as they were several billion years ago. How much does this matter? It will be remembered that, according to Lemaître's theory, all the galaxies were formed at more or less the same time, and that no new galaxies are forming now. Therefore all galaxies have more or less the same birthday on the basis of this theory. If we look at very distant

FIG. 11. *The Lemaître (A & B) and steady-state (1 & 2) theories contrasted: In Lemaître's theory all the galaxies were born close to each other (A) some ten thousand million years ago. Since then they have been growing up and drifting apart, and now we have old galaxies (B) with vast distances between them. In the steady-state theory new galaxies (1) are being born all the time. As the old galaxies get farther and farther away from each other, the new ones (2) form in the spaces between.*

ones, we see them when the light that we now receive was emitted by them. On the other hand, near galaxies we see more or less as they are now. An analogy is given by a pair of twins born in England, but separated at an early stage, one of them staying in England, the other going to Australia. If pictures of the Australian twin are frequently sent by surface mail to the home of the other one, then on the photographs the Australian one will persistently look several weeks younger than the English one because of the delay in the mails. Similarly, we have the delay in the mails in the universe, the mails being represented by the light that comes to us from these distant regions. Accordingly, the distant galaxies should look younger to us than the near ones on the basis of Lemaître's theory. Unfortunately, we do not know what a young galaxy looks like compared with an old one. Our theories of the evolution of galaxies have not got far enough. But we may reasonably expect that they look different in some way.

FIG. 12.  *If we look far enough into space, we can see galaxies as they were thousands of millions of years ago. For instance, our own galaxy is pictured at A with our sun at B. At C are pictured the nearest galaxies whose light takes about ten million years to reach us. But at the right (D) light from the most distant galaxies takes thousands of millions of years to reach us. In reality we see them as they were long, long ago.*

Young galaxies may be more or less sociable than old ones; that is to say, they may cluster rather more or rather less. They may have different shapes or colors, and there are many other characteristics that might well be different in a young galaxy from what they are in an old one. If, then, one looks out into space and compares the features of distant galaxies and of near ones, then any visible difference would be ascribed to the fact that one saw the distant galaxies at an earlier stage of their lives than the near ones. In the model of the steady-state theory, the situation is quite different. For in that model the universe always presents the same aspect. Galaxies are being born all the time. In distant regions the average age of galaxies is the same as in near regions, and thus they look just the same. In our analogy of the twins, if the Australian friend sent a picture of a collection of young children in Australia, then this collection would not look any younger than a similar collection in England, in spite of the delay in the mails. In the Australian collection, just as in the English, there would be children of all ages. Accordingly, if the steady-state theory is correct, none of the average features of galaxies should change with distance. And so here we have our first test —to see whether any of the features of galaxies varies with distance. If there is such a variation, then it is in flagrant contradiction with the steady-state theory and that theory has been shot down. If there is no variation, we cannot be similarly certain that the evolutionary theories have been shot down, because it may just be that we cannot see far enough to notice any such variation. However, absence of variation to a really large distance would make us rather suspicious of evolutionary theories.

## The Evolution of Galaxies

Another test concerns the number of galaxies of more than a given brightness. To measure the distance of individual galaxies is an exceedingly difficult and almost impossible task for the astronomer. But he can make estimates of their distances by seeing how bright they look. The fainter a galaxy looks, the greater he will suspect its distance to be. In the evolutionary universe, when we look at distant regions and see them as they were a long time ago, we should see the galaxies there much closer together than they are now, owing to the expansion of the universe that has been going on since the light was sent out. On the basis of the steady-state theory, the density of galaxies and their average distances apart were the same then as they are now, in spite of the expansion, simply because many of the galaxies now in existence had not been born then. Therefore, there should be many more faint (i.e., distant) galaxies according to evolutionary theories than according to the steady-state theory. Again here is a possible avenue of testing. It is quite likely that it will be more fruitful to

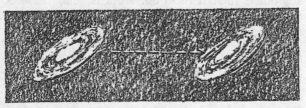

FIG. 13. *At the present time galaxies have a certain size (about 80,000 light-years in diameter) and are a certain average distance (about one and a half million light-years) apart.*

51

carry out these tests with a radio telescope rather than with an optical one.

Other tests concern the formation of galaxies. In the steady-state theory, galaxies must be forming all the time in the space between existing galaxies so as to keep up the average density of galaxies in spite of the expansion of the universe. One is, therefore, interested in the formation of galaxies in the presence of existing ones. In evolutionary theories, on the other hand, there was a period before there were any galaxies. The question then arises of the formation of the first of all galaxies. Both of these problems are questions for the theoretical worker. He must try to see in what conditions galaxies can form. If it were to turn out that galaxies can only form in the presence of existing galaxies, then we would be back to the old question of which came first—chicken or egg? But this question holds no terrors for the steady-state theory, for in that theory the universe has been going on for an infinite time and has never changed or the large scale; hence, we are not worried by the reference to the previous generation. On the other hand, the evolutionary theories are entirely dependent on the possibility of the formation of galaxies before there were any others to start them off. Work is going on in both these problems, and we may well hope for enlightenment from the theoreticians before very long.

## Origin of the Elements

Next there is the problem of the origin of the elements. From the point of view of the nuclear physicist, hydrogen is by far the simplest element. It also happens on a large scale to be by far the most common of all elements. For a long time people have suspected that hydrogen was in fact the origin of all matter and that, in some way, the other elements had been built up out of hydrogen. As far as the next simplest element, helium, is concerned, there is no difficulty about this, as helium is synthesized from hydrogen in stars all the time. But where do all the many other elements come from? For a long time it seemed that none of the stars we knew was hot enough even at its center to have been the source of any of the more complicated elements. It is reported that when Sir Arthur S. Eddington, the famous English astronomer and cosmologist, was told by the nuclear physicists that the temperatures he had calculated for the centers of the stars were quite insufficient to build up any elements more complicated than helium, he replied, "Then I wish the nuclear physicists would go to a much hotter place."

The search for this "hotter place" went on for quite some time. With Lemaître's model, which has a very hot, dense state at the beginning, many people thought that this "much hotter place" had been found. However, this is not a situation that the steady-state theory can accept. According to this theory, the universe is much the same at all times. If there are no factories *now* in existence in which heavy elements can be made, then there *never* were any such factories. Accordingly, attempts were made to find these factories in the existing universe. And, indeed, they were found. They seem to be of two different kinds, and they are both important. One is the centers of the enormously large stars referred to as red giants. These stars are really quite enormous, with radii a hundred times or more that of the sun. According to modern ideas, at their centers conditions are suitable for the building up of many heavy elements and the theory also says that many of these stars eventually explode and so obligingly scatter the newly formed elements all over space. They are not only a factory for making these elements but a retail distribution channel as well that makes them available universally.

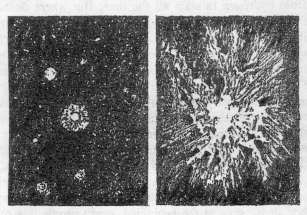

FIG. 14. *Occasionally we see explosions in space when a star flares up with intense brilliancy thousands of millions of times greater than that of our sun. From calculations we can deduce the temperatures in these exploding stars. There is sufficient heat to combine lighter elements and thereby produce the heavier ones.*

Other sources are the extraordinary stars known as supernovae. These are stars that suddenly flare up to enormous brilliance, thousands of millions of times the brightness of the sun, and then gradually fade away. They are often observed in other galaxies, though in each galaxy they seem to occur only once every few hundred years. In our own galaxy a few of them are known to have occurred in historical times and have been described. The most famous of them is the celebrated Chinese supernova of A.D. 1054. The Chinese left us a very full description of the magnificent spectacle presented by a star so bright as to be visible in daytime. It gradually faded, and now, 900 years later, we can see with a telescope the remains of the explosion as a diffuse cloud of gas known as the Crab Nebula. These supernovae also are factories and distribution channels for heavy elements, which are formed in the course of this gigantic outburst and then scattered all over space. There is now good reason to believe that, with these sources that have been thoroughly investigated, we can fully account for the existence of all the chemical elements by means of types of stars that can actually be observed at present. With this, much of the attraction of the very hot and dense initial state of Lemaître's model has gone; and, indeed, the physicists say now that, in any case, it could not have produced the elements.

There are many other tests which are too technical to be described here. Enough has been said, however, to show that our current theories are not merely idle speculations but are used for the purpose of making forecasts that can be shot down or, at least, shot at, by observers.

# V. The Stars

There can be few places in the whole universe as inaccessible to us as the centers of the stars. Even the most imaginative space traveler can hardly consider a trip to the center of a star, nor does there seem to be any chance of getting light or other information out from there directly. Nevertheless, the theory of what goes on in the interior of the stars is particularly well developed, and we have a great deal of confidence in it. How does this situation come about? It is the purpose of the theory of stellar constitution, like that of any other scientific theory, to link up the different items of information we have got. The information we have got about the stars necessarily refers to the outside of the stars. Nevertheless, it turns out that enough information can be found from observations of the outsides of the stars to enable us to make confident statements about their interiors. What, then, are the observable features of the outsides of the stars that are relevant to the study of the constitution of the stars?

The first thing one notices about a star is that it shines. The intensity of light we receive from a star can be measured and this is called its apparent luminosity. The word "apparent" here refers to the fact that this is not the true or intrinsic luminosity of the star. It is not the rate at which the star sends out light, but the rate at which we receive it, which naturally depends very much on the distance of the star from us and on any possible obscuring clouds of matter between the star and us.

FIG. 15. *Naturally the star of chief interest to the dwellers on earth is our own sun—a great flaming gaseous sphere 864,000 miles in diameter—whose physical characteristics are a fiery gaseous core whose temperature is 13,000,000 degrees C. Outside the core is a glowing zone and outside that the blazing turbulent outer surface which we see (6000 degrees C). (Our earth, approximately to scale, is the small white speck in the upper right corner.)*

Therefore, before our measurement of the apparent luminosity of a star tells us anything about its intrinsic or absolute luminosity (which alone is information about the star itself), we must have some way of ascertaining the distance of the star.

## Distances of the Stars: Parallax

How is the distance of a star measured? The most reliable method which, unfortunately, can be applied only to the few hundred nearest stars is that of the so-called trigonometric parallax. In spite of the forbidding name, the idea of it is quite simple. If you sit in a room some way from the window and look out through the window and then move your head a little, the window frame will obscure first one and then another part of the view. In other words, owing to the motion of your head the near object—the window frame—is first in line with some part of the view, and then with another. In astronomy, unfortunately, moving one's head is not enough.

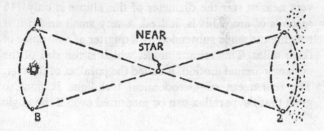

NEAR STAR

FIG. 16. *Distance is measured by the parallax method. A near star is in line with a particular distant star at one time of the year (1) and with another (2) six months later when the earth has moved (from B to A) about the sun. The difference in the direction of the rays from the near star determines its distance.*

All the stars are too far away for a small movement like that to have any effect at all. However, we are all on the earth and therefore moving round the sun, covering quite a substantial distance in the course of six months. Six months from now we will be 190 million miles away from where we are today, though a year from now we will be back again where we are today. If, then, some stars are very much nearer than most others, in the course of the year the apparent position of these near stars relative to the distant ones will change. In fact, every near star will seem to describe a small ellipse against the background of distant stars.

In favorable circumstances, the astronomer can observe this apparent annual motion of a near star against the background of distant stars. When he can do so, then he can measure the size of this elliptical annual motion and, with the aid of a little trigonometry, he can thus determine the distance of the nearest star. Unfortunately, stars are so far away from us that even for the very nearest star the diameter of this ellipse is only 1½ seconds of arc. This is, indeed, a very small angle; it is roughly the angle subtended by a quarter at a distance of three miles. This minute angle, which is the size of the apparent annual motion, is called the parallax of the star. The refinement of astronomical technique is now so great that the parallax can be measured even if the angle

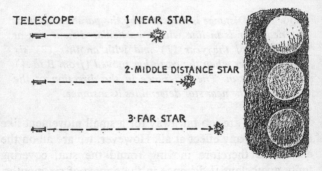

FIG. 17. *Though equal amounts of light are sent out by these three stars, which are of the same luminosity, the amount received diminishes with increase in distance. If the astronomer has already determined the distance, he can use the observed brightness to determine the luminosity of the star; that is, the near star will be bright and the far star dim.*

subtended by the apparent annual motion of a star is only around a tenth of a second of arc, that is, the size of a quarter at a distance of forty miles. In this way, the distances of several hundred stars have been measured. Incidentally, if the diameter of the ellipse subtends one second of arc, then the distance of the star from us is so great that light takes six years to get from the star to us. The nearest star is at a distance of about four light-years.

If the parallax of a star is known, then one knows its distance and, supposing there to be no obscuring matter between the star and us (as, indeed, seems to be the case for most stars for which a trigonometric parallax is known) then one can immediately infer from its apparent luminosity its absolute or intrinsic luminosity—the rate at which the star sends out light.

## Color and Temperature

The next item of information about a star comes from an examination of its light by the spectroscope. What one is really after here is nothing more complicated than the color of the star. For the color tells us what the temperature of the surface is. It is a remarkable fact that for a glowing, opaque object the color of the glow is independent of the composition of the body; it depends only on its temperature. We are all familiar with this. If you look into a nice, glowing coal fire and stick a hot poker in and wait until it has heated up, then at the back of the fire the glowing piece of coal, the glowing firebrick and the glowing poker all look so much alike in color that it is only by their shapes that we can distinguish one from the other. Indeed, the colors are so much alike that it is difficult to see where one ends and the other begins. Moreover, we are familiar with the fact that the actual color of the glow depends on the temperature. If the heat is not very great, the color is a deep red; if the fire is rather hotter, we have a bright red, or even an orange glow; with the very hottest fires, we may get a yellow color. Higher temperatures than these are not normally achieved in domestic fires, but in industrial processes or in the laboratory one knows that beyond yellow heat comes white heat, and for yet higher temperature the white takes on a bluish tinge. Not only can one link the color of the glow with the temperature of the body emitting it in a way which is quite independent of the composition of that body, but one also knows that, with a given color of glow, that is, with a given temperature, the intensity of radiation and heat emission is completely definite. One knows that a dull, red poker does not emit nearly as much heat as a bright red or yellow one; that a fire that is really hot and looks yellow radiates very much more into the room than a fire that is only just glowing. The physicist can measure how much comes out of the glowing body in the form of light and heat. He finds that the emission per unit surface is, again, quite independent of the composition of the body, but depends very much on the temperature. In fact, it goes with the fourth power of the absolute temperature. That means that doubling the temperature increases the rate of emission of heat by a factor 16.

The property that a body radiates heat from its surface also applies at much lower temperatures where no glow is visible. Indeed, even at perfectly ordinary temperatures everything radiates. In fact, we ourselves—our own bodies—lose a good deal of heat by radiating to our surroundings more than we receive from them. It is estimated that, in ordinary circumstances, about half the loss of bodily heat is by radiation, the other half being given to the surrounding air. Indeed, radiation is one of the major problems in domestic heating. The amount of radiation we receive depends on the temperature of our surroundings, that is, the walls, ceilings and floors of the rooms we live in. If these are cold, then even if the air in the room is at a high temperature (so that our total loss of heat is not excessive) we yet feel uncomfortable and call the room stuffy, for it is disagreeable to lose a lot of heat by radiation and little to the air. Of course, if we keep a room heated night and day, then the air will gradually heat up the walls, we will receive more radiation from them, and conditions of comfort will return. Another way of achieving comfort is to put something opaque between us and the cold places. We all know how much warmer it makes the feel of a room to draw a curtain across a window on a cold day. For then the heat radiation reaches us, not from the windowpane which is cooled by contact with the

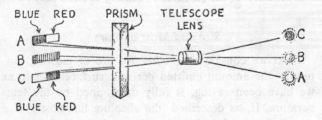

FIG. 18. *The temperature of a star can be determined from the color of the star. In the diagram the light from star A shown passing through the prism is primarily blue and therefore the star is a "hot" star. Star B shows continuous color change from blue to red and is therefore of an intermediate temperature, while star C is a red star and "cool."*

outside air, but from the curtain which is warmed by the interior air of the room. Hanging tapestries on walls was an old way of improving comfort conditions in a room; underfloor heating and ceiling heating are modern ways of achieving the same end and keeping the radiation balance of our bodies in agreeable equilibrium.

To return now to the stars, their light does not reach us directly from the opaque surfaces of the stars (the place where the stellar material becomes so dense that it is no longer transparent), but it has to pass through the gases of the stellar atmospheres surrounding stars before it reaches us. In this way, the extremely complicated dark lines of the stellar spectra are produced; though no doubt these contain a wealth of information, it has proved exceedingly difficult to unravel it. However, the astronomer can classify the spectra of the stars by these lines and can define various types of stars in this way. It is these spectral types that are related to the surface temperature; and, indeed, it is in this manner that the temperature of the surfaces is usually determined.

## Size and Mass of Stars

Next we consider the other feature of glowing materials—the amount emitted per unit surface—which, as we have been saying, is fully determined by the temperature. If, as described, the absolute luminosity of a star has been found and the temperature of its surface, then one knows not only how much light the star sends out altogether, but also how much light it emits per unit surface, namely, the amount corresponding to its temperature. Therefore, by division one can find the total surface area of the star. Assuming the star to be spherical in shape, one can immediately calculate its radius. Thus, we have the remarkable result that although even in the biggest telescopes the size of a star does not show up, yet in this indirect fashion it has been possible to determine the radii of numerous stars.

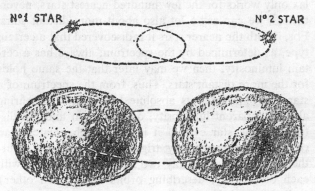

N°1 STAR    N°2 STAR

FIG. 19. *Many stars are known as binaries, that is, two stars revolving about each other under the influence of each other's gravitational attraction. Some are far apart and slowly circle about each other in hundreds of years. Other types of binary stars almost touch as they circle each other at speeds in excess of 100,000 miles an hour. They are rendered oval by the attractive forces of each other. In many cases the astronomer can observe the orbits of these stars with sufficient accuracy to enable him to evaluate the gravitational attraction of the stars which—with Newton's Law of Gravitation—tells him the magnitude of their masses.*

A third observable characteristic is the mass of the stars, at least in quite a few cases. The astronomer makes use of the fact that many stars are binaries, that is, pairs of stars, orbiting about each other under mutual gravitational pull. If the orbit can be observed with sufficient accuracy, then it is frequently possible to determine the masses of the two stars. Thus, for many stars three characteristics are known—the absolute luminosity; the spectral type or, equivalently, the surface temperature; and the mass. Although the method of trigonometric parallax only works for the few hundred nearest stars, nevertheless, we can say a lot also about more distant stars. For, if with the nearer stars it is discovered that a certain type, as determined by the spectrum, always has a certain luminosity, then we may infer that the same holds for the more distant stars. Thus, from the spectrum of a star, one can infer its absolute luminosity. Measuring also its apparent luminosity, one can then find the distance of the star even if it is very much greater than could be determined by trigonometric parallax. Furthermore, if in some way two stars are associated with each other (say, describing orbits about each other) and we can infer the distance of one of them in the manner just described, then the distance of the other one follows because they must be close together. In this way, one can find out a great deal even about types of stars not represented among the few hundred nearest stars that are accessible to the method of trigonometric parallax. Thus, luminosity and radius are known for a large number of stars, and for quite a few of them the mass has also been determined.

# VI.  What Goes on inside the Stars

In the previous chapter it was described how absolute luminosity and surface temperature and, therefore, radius, come to be known for a large number of stars, and how for quite a few other stars the mass, too, has been determined. The next question to investigate is whether these different characteristics are related to each other. For this purpose we draw a diagram, in which we represent the surface temperature and the absolute luminosity for each star for which these characteristics are known. This is referred to as a Hertzsprung-Russell diagram, after the first two astronomers (Professors E. Hertzsprung, of Leyden, and H. N. Russell, of Cambridge) who constructed it. Such a diagram is illustrated in Fig. 20. Each star is represented as a point. The cooler the star is, the farther the representative point is to the right; the hotter, the farther it is to the left. Hence all red stars appear toward the right of the diagram; yellow stars neither right nor left but in the middle, and white, or bluish-white stars on the left. The greater the intrinsic luminosity of a star is, that is, the more light it sends out, the higher up it appears on the diagram. The brightest stars appear near the top; the faintest ones near the foot of the diagram. It is then observed that the large majority of stars lie in a broad band reaching from the bottom right-hand corner (faint red stars) to the top left-hand corner (bright blue stars).

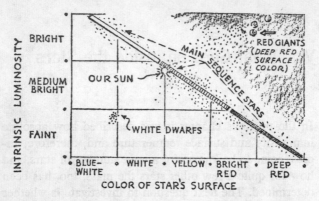

FIG. 20. *In previous chapters it has been explained how the astronomer gets to know the luminosity and surface temperature of stars and arrive at their radius and sometimes their mass. Next he has to determine how these different characteristics are related, so he has to produce diagrams such as were first made by the astronomers Hertzsprung and Russell in order to correlate the surface temperature and absolute luminosity.*

## Red Giants, White Dwarfs and the Main Sequence

This band of stars is known as the main sequence, and any star belonging to this band is referred to as a main-sequence star. Our own sun is a main-sequence star and appears roughly in the middle of the diagram. Stretching from a point on the main sequence, a little above the sun to the top right-hand corner, we have another family of stars. These stars are called Red Giants. As these stars appear so high in the diagram they are very bright stars; they send out a large amount of heat and light. However, they are only red, that is to say, their surface temperature is not high. Accordingly, not much

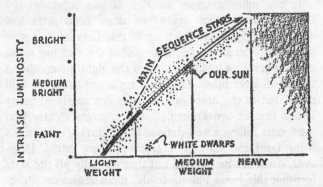

heat or light is emitted per unit area of surface on such a star. In order to make up the total emission the whole surface area of these stars must be immense. They are greatly distended stars. Some of them have a radius a hundred times the radius of the sun, which itself is a hundred times the radius of the earth. Finally, we notice a group of stars toward the bottom left-hand corner. These are called the White Dwarfs and they are in every respect the opposite of the Red Giants. They do not emit much light altogether, but the surface is white-hot and so emits a lot of heat and light per unit area. Accordingly, the total surface area must be small, and these objects are tiny by comparison with other stars. Their radius is often not much larger than the radius of the earth. There are other, rarer types of stars which will not be referred to here. It may, however, be worth mentioning that fully investigated stars form a somewhat unrepresentative collection, because a bright star is visible over a very much larger distance than a faint star. Thus, our information about bright stars has been gained from a much larger region than our knowledge of faint ones, and so the bright ones are greatly overrepresented.

In the other diagram of Fig. 20 we represent the stellar masses. Once again, we draw faint stars low down and bright stars high up in the diagram; but now the position near the left means that the star has small mass, whereas a position toward the right means that a star has a large mass. This diagram is not nearly so well populated as the other one because not nearly so many stellar masses are known. But it emerges clearly that most stars follow a well-defined band, stars of small mass being faint and stars of large mass being bright. However, it should be pointed out that virtually all the stars forming this band belong to the main sequence. Probably because of their vast extent, Red Giants do not usually have companions, and so almost no masses are known for them. White Dwarfs seem to lie definitely below the band.

## The Structure of Stars

What can the theory of stellar structure tell us about all these bodies and their characteristics, as shown in Figs. 21 and 22? First, the theory shows us that we have to distinguish sharply between the White Dwarfs and all other stars. In all other stars the material behaves virtually throughout the star as a gas, that is, as a highly compressible medium in which temperature, density and pressure are related as in an ordinary gas such as, say, the air. However, owing to the enormous pressures in the interiors of stars, the density of the material is very large compared with the density of gases as we know them in our surroundings. For example, the density of air is not much more than one part in a thousand of that of water; but the mean density of the sun is 1.4 times that of water. It is a ridiculous but curious thought

FIG. 21. *The heat is produced in the blazing center (A) of a star and passes outward through the gaseous transporting shell (B) and finally radiates from the surface (C) as light.*

FIG. 22. *The surface of a star is always in blazing agitation caused by the heat from its interior. From time to time mighty flaming eruptions gush up for thousands of miles and drop back onto the surface when they have cooled.*

71

that, if one put the sun on an ocean large enough to hold it and forgot about its steam-raising properties, then it would sink. Naturally, the density at the surface of the sun is much lower than at the center, where it may reach the colossal figure of eighty or a hundred times that of water, about eight times as heavy as lead. It is, indeed, remarkable that material can be so highly compressed and yet behave as a gas. This gaseous behavior at enormous densities is, to some extent, due to the very high temperatures prevailing in the centers of the stars—temperatures of ten million degrees centigrade or more.

The fact that the centers of the stars are so very much hotter than the surfaces leads to a flow of energy from the central regions to the outer parts. It is this flow that, on emerging into space on the surface of the star, forms the radiation of heat and light by which the star is seen. Allowing for the fact that the theorist must always bear in mind the tremendous gravitational pull of the star on its own matter, the problem he faces can conveniently be divided into two parts: First; the problem of the transport of heat from the central regions to the surface, and secondly, the generation of heat in the central regions. It was, again, one of Eddington's remarkable discoveries that the problem could be so divided and that useful information could be gained from the solution of the first problem alone. This was of great importance for the development of the subject because though means were at hand to solve this problem in the mid-twenties, the problem of energy generation required an understanding of nuclear physics that was not available until 1938. Eddington was able to show that, if the composition of the star was the same throughout, that is to say, if the distribution of chemical elements was uniform throughout the star, then the flow of energy demanded that there should be a relation between that mass, luminosity and radius in which the radius played a completely subordinate part, so subordinate that one could often forget about it. In this way he derived his famous mass-luminosity relation that fits the observed curve very well indeed. His theory also enabled him to infer the central temperature of the stars. The remarkable result he obtained was that there was very little variation in central temperature from one main-sequence star to any other. This result puzzled him very much because he correctly supposed that the rate of nuclear energy production depended on temperature, and the energy requirements of different stars differ greatly. In a celebrated phrase he asked: Does matter release energy at as definite a temperature as water releases steam at boiling point?

## Answering Eddington's Question

It needed much progress in nuclear physics before this problem could be solved. The first remarkable point to be clear about is how very little energy per unit mass is actually liberated in stars. The amount of average solar matter required to produce as much light and heat as a small (40-watt) electric light bulb is 200 tons. This may be compared with a human being whose heat output is more than a hundred watts, even when sitting down. The enormous brilliance of the sun is only due to the fact that it is so very deep. Behind every square foot of its surface there lies a tremendous depth of matter, the distance from the center to the surface being 440,000 miles. All the energy released in this region can flow out into space only through the surface. We understand now the nuclear reactions that actually produce the energy in the stars. They are all concerned with the transmutation of hydrogen into helium. At the temperatures prevailing at the centers of the stars the hydrogen nuclei (protons), stripped of their electrons by the heat motion, rush about and frequently collide with each other. The vast majority of the collisions are not so hard as to lead to any noticeable result, but every now and then (one collision out of every thousand million million million to be precise) the collision is extra hard and happens, as it were, to hit a vital spot; and then the two protons do not separate but stick together to form a deuteron. It

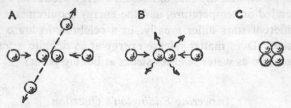

FIG. 23. *Thermonuclear fusion produces heat when two protons collide and stick together (B) instead of bouncing off each other (A). Occasionally four protons adhere and produce more heat. Two of them turn into neutrons and thus a helium nucleus is formed.*

is then relatively easy for the deuteron to participate in more nuclear reactions which lead eventually to the formation of a helium nucleus. This contains effectively four protons, though two of them have changed to neutrons. The energy obtained in such a transmutation is tremendous. One gram of hydrogen turned into helium liberates nearly 200,000 kilowatt hours. The rate at which this energy is released depends very critically on temperature, though not quite so critically as the boiling of water.

## The Burning of Hydrogen

If our knowledge of these nuclear transmutations is added to the solution of the transport problem, one finds that for a chemically homogeneous star not only are mass and luminosity related in the way Eddington found, but there is also a relation between luminosity and radius, and, therefore, surface temperature, such as corresponds to a main-sequence star. The fit of the theoretical predictions and the observed characteristics of the stars is particularly good if these stars are supposed not only to be chemically homogeneous but to contain almost pure hydrogen with just a small admixture of other elements. We have, therefore, obtained a perfect picture of a main-sequence star fitting the known examples in every respect. It is most comforting that the simplest theoretical model—the homogeneous gaseous star—should fit the most common type—the main-sequence star.

We have to consider more complicated models to fit the less common stars—the Red Giants and the White Dwarfs. Can these complications arise in a natural way? The nuclear reactions that convert hydrogen into helium and so keep a star supplied with energy depend very much on the temperature. The higher the temperature the faster they go on. Since the center of a star is much hotter than any other place in it, it follows that the reactions will occur effectively only in the central regions. In the course of time, therefore, the hydrogen at the center will at least partly be turned into helium, whereas in the outer regions of the star the hydrogen will be unaffected. Accordingly, a chemical inhomogeneity will develop in the star, central regions becoming helium-

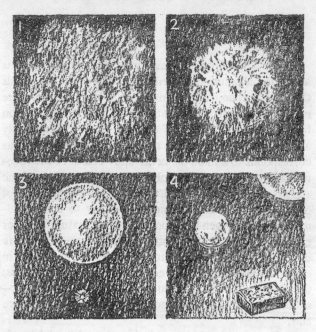

FIG. 24. *A star is born (1) from a shapeless gas cloud, consisting mainly of hydrogen. As it contracts, its center gradually gets hotter and eventually becomes a star. It becomes spherical (2) and contracts still more because of the gravitational attraction among all the particles of the star. The fusion of hydrogen into helium generates more heat in the center. In time the center becomes mostly helium surrounded by a thick shell of hydrogen (3). The star increases so tremendously in size that the supply of heat can maintain the outer surface only at a much lower temperature, hence the red color and the name Red Giant. Our sun drawn to scale is the small white spot below the Red Giant. Since the helium core cannot produce heat, the Red Giant gradually contracts to the point where the heat in the core*

rich, whereas the rest continues to be almost pure hydrogen. It can then be shown that eventually this inhomogeneity will lead to a change in the structure of the star and to a great increase of radius. In other words, the star will become a Red Giant. This development will occur sooner for the massive stars, because they burn up the hydrogen very much faster. Therefore, this great extension of radius—this transition to the Red Giant type—will occur first among the most massive and, therefore, brightest stars. If no star in our galaxy is more than eight or ten thousand million years old, then the Red Giants will be confined to the bright stars as, indeed, they are. Although much remains to be done before all the Red Giants are as fully understood as the main-sequence stars, the situation is not unsatisfactory.

What about the White Dwarf stars? Very bright stars, as time goes on, will burn up more and more of the hydrogen, and eventually they will be left without any hydrogen. Later developments are quite complicated but one can see that in due course such stars will be unable to maintain their heat balance. They will begin to cool and to shrink. It turns out that as long as the star remains a pure gas, there is no limit to the shrinkage. However, the material eventually becomes so dense that the constituent particles become tightly packed. It then becomes very hard to compress them any more, and so the material has ceased to behave like a gas. It is at this stage that the star presents the appearance of a White Dwarf.

---

*can maintain the surface of the now small star at a very high temperature. These White Dwarfs are very small compared with our sun, shown in the upper right corner, and exceedingly dense, such that a piece of a White Dwarf the size of a matchbox would weigh over two tons.*

The material has been compacted as far as it will go. It has attained the required strength by being so terribly dense. There are certain predictions one can make about the White Dwarf state, in particular that the mass can only be fairly small. Any excess mass must somehow have been thrown off into space in outbursts before the White Dwarf stage was reached. The predictions of the theory fit all the known White Dwarfs well. It should not, however, be thought that all problems of stellar constitution have been solved. There are various peculiar types of stars that are still mysterious in their behavior.

# VII. Between the Stars

The stars are the great lighthouses of space. We can see them over tremendous distances, and they look prominent and remarkable objects to us. To a sailor, passing a coast at night, lighthouses are not only the most useful, but also the most prominent objects that he sees. However, we all know that he would be grossly mistaken if he thought that the lighthouses were all there was to the land. Similarly, we may be in danger of overrating the importance of the stars just because they are so very bright and so easily visible, and we may be neglecting whatever else there may be in space. How can we find out anything about the regions between the stars? First of all, we must realize that most parts of space are transparent. If they were not transparent then, of course, we wouldn't be able to see stars at all. This is rather negative evidence, for there can be lots of materials in space that would not make it opaque. In particular, there can be vast amounts of hydrogen gas in the enormous spaces between the stars, and they can yet be so tenuous that they would not intercept any of the light passing through. In some regions of the sky we see patches without stars surrounded by regions full of stars. This occurs particularly in the Milky Way, and the only plausible explanation for this fact is that these dark patches are opaque clouds of gas intercepting the light of the stars behind them. One of the best known of these is the aptly named Coal Sack in the Milky Way. There are numerous other places like that where obviously a dark cloud in-

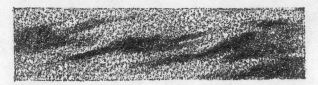

FIG. 25. *Though the stars by their brightness seem to populate the sky, there are considerable gaps—shown as dark regions—where no star appears. These are great areas where vast clouds of interstellar dust obscure the view.*

terferes with the light of the stars behind it. How can we find out more about these clouds of matter? It would seem plausible that if space is quite transparent in some regions and completely opaque in others, it should be in an intermediate stage, that is, foggy, in yet other parts. How would such fogginess show itself to the astronomer? Let us try to explore this question by thinking of examples from the earth.

## Cosmic Haze

At sunset the rays of the sun pass through very much more of the low atmosphere to reach us than they do when the sun is high in the sky. This has the effect, known to us all, that at sunset the sun looks very much redder than its ordinary appearance. Often this is a very beautiful spectacle. Also we know that on a foggy night there often appears a halo surrounding the moon which is due to the diffraction of the light of the moon by the particles making up the fog. Frequently when the astronomer looks at a star, he can recognize its type from its spectral lines. He knows then what color he would expect the star to show if nothing interfered with its light on its

PLATE V. *A photograph of a cluster of galaxies in* Corona Borealis—*several of which are clearly visible here*—*about 500 million light-years away.*

PLATE VI.   *A cluster of galaxies in* Hydra, *1500 million light-years away. The numerous diffuse objects are galaxies forming part of a cluster. The clear objects are stars near to us.*

PLATE VII.  *A photograph of a field of faint galaxies in the constellation of* Pisces *at a distance of well over a billion light-years.*

PLATE VIII.    *A spiral galaxy seen edge-on. The dark ring is a belt of dust obscuring the light of the stars behind it.*

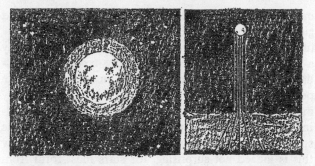

FIG. 26. *The moon when viewed through light fog appears with a halo, which is caused by the moon's rays being deflected by fog particles.*

journey to him. But quite often a star looks redder than that, particularly if it is a very distant star, in the plane of the Milky Way. The conclusion is clear. The light of the star is reddened by an intervening haze of matter, just as the light of the sun is reddened by the haze in the atmosphere at sunset. A close study, by means of the spectroscope, of the effects on the light of the star of the passage through the cloud may enable the astronomer to find out what the cloud consists of, or at least to discover what some of its constituents are. It appears that many clouds contain dust not unlike the dust we know on the earth, with calcium and carbon and similar elements represented. It is cold in space, and frozen grains of methane are not infrequent. The halo effect is also familiar. The picture of the so-called Owl Nebula (Plate XII) shows a cloud of gas illuminated by a star behind it. Sometimes also clouds impinge on each other with high velocity, and then, by the enormous friction, some parts of the cloud begin to glow. Possibly shock waves, such as we get on the earth after an explosion, may also be responsible in space for making a cloud glow on occasions. A beautiful example of this is the filamentary nebula shown in Fig. 27. If there were only a few clouds about, one could hardly expect to see collisions between them or find a star in such a fortunate position as to illuminate a whole cloud. From the many instances of these effects that we know, we can accordingly infer how very much matter there must be in the space between the stars. From a theoretical point of view this is indeed not surprising, for stars must form from such diffuse matter and grow by swallowing it up.

FIG. 27. *Some clouds of dust and other matter impinge upon each other at high speed and, by the enormous friction set up, some parts of the cloud glow and produce the beautiful effect as seen in this picture of a filamentary nebula.*

### Polarization of Light

Another piece of evidence about what goes on in the space between the stars has been discovered only relatively recently. This is the polarization of starlight. What is polarization, and how can we find it? Light has a number of familiar properties. It travels in straight lines with a definite velocity; it has intensity, that is, brightness, and it may show any of many colors or a combination of them. But this does not exhaust the characteristics of light, though the remaining one, polarization, is rather more difficult to observe. There is a direction associated with light, a direction that is invariably at right angles to the direction of propagation, and is called the direction of polarization. Most materials cannot distinguish between light that is polarized in different directions; but certain crystals and other materials are transparent to one direction of polarization and opaque to the other.

If, then, we take two such crystals and shine a beam of light through them, the first crystal will select from all the light in the beam only that which is associated with a particular direction in the crystal. We may imagine each particle of light, as it were, carrying a stick normal to the direction of propagation. The crystal then acts as a fence with long bars parallel to each other and the light that carries sticks at right angles to these bars can't get through; whereas the light that carries its sticks parallel to the bars manages to pass through. If the second crystal is held parallel to the first, then all the light that passed through the first one will go through the second one. If, on the other hand, the second crystal is held at right angles to the first one, then none of the light will come through at all, for the direction of the stick that managed to get through the first fence is just the direction that is unable to get through the second fence, since the directions of the posts of the two fences are at right angles to each other. Although crystals show this polarization phenomenon far more strongly than anything else we come across in ordinary life, yet there are some occasions where polarization matters. Mostly we deal with light which is unpolarized; that is to say, the sticks that the individual particles carry are in all sorts of directions, some in one direction, some in another.

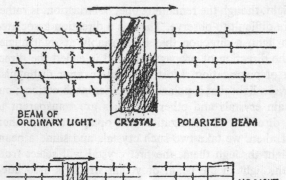

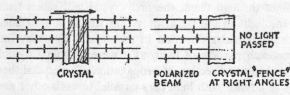

FIG. 28. *Light travels in straight lines at a definite velocity, but it also has an oscillating motion at right angles to the direction of travel. Certain crystals polarize light, that is, transmit only light whose sidewise motion is in a certain direction. If this light is passed through a second crystal oriented in the same direction as the first, all the light will be transmitted. If a third crystal in the light path is turned at 90 degrees to the second, no light will be transmitted.*

The direction of polarization of the light, as it were, is not ordered. Among the few phenomena where it does matter is glare. If an almost horizontal beam of light is reflected by a wet surface such as a wet road, then the horizontal direction of polarization is much more strongly reflected than the vertical one. Therefore, the glare of the headlights of other cars or of street lights reflected in the road is predominantly horizontally polarized. That is to say, the sticks carried by the particles of light reflected from the road are, in the main, horizontal. If we look at the picture through a crystal passing only vertically polarized light, then far less of the glare will come through the crystal than of other light. In this lies the advantage of using a polarizer as glasses for night driving in wet conditions.

## Polarized Starlight

Polarization occurs also in other ways, especially in short radio waves. This is the reason why TV aerials have to be vertical, and Very High Frequency sound aerials have to be horizontal. The transmitter in the one case transmits only horizontally polarized radio waves; in the other, only vertically polarized ones. If, now, the astronomer looks at the light of the stars and tries to discover whether it is polarized—that is to say, whether more of the particles of light carry sticks pointing in one direction than in another—then he finds that indeed the light of some stars is quite noticeably polarized. In particular, he finds that for many of the stars whose light is reddened by passing through a fog of interstellar matter,

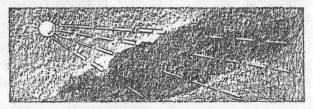

FIG. 29. *Some of the gas clouds in space, like certain crystals, polarize light—that is, transmit only that light whose sidewise motion is in a certain direction.*

this polarization is quite appreciable, so that a few per cent more light carries sticks of one direction than in the other. How is this remarkable modern discovery to be explained? It is very difficult to understand how a star as a whole can send out polarized rather than unpolarized light. Combining this with the fact that it is just the light that has passed through a lot of interstellar fog that shows the polarization most noticeably, we may presume that it occurs in the passage through interstellar matter. But how can it occur there? Interstellar matter is certainly not a crystal. It isn't as though we looked at the stars through enormous lined up crystals floating in space. Interstellar matter is just dust and gas. Gas certainly cannot polarize anything, but what about dust? Here the analogy of the fence helps again.

Suppose the individual particles of dust are rather long and thin rods, like iron filings, for example. Then if they are all aligned—that is to say, they are all parallel—they, just like the fence, will pass more light with the direction of polarization parallel to the rods than light carrying sticks normal to the direction of the rods. We are, therefore, led to believe that some, at least, of the interstellar dust may consist of rodlike particles. But how do they come to be aligned? This is not an easy question to answer, but what springs to mind immediately are the familiar pictures of how iron filings may be aligned by the action of a magnet; and, indeed, it is not easy to think of any other cause for aligning the dust particles in the spaces between the stars. A magnetic field seems to be the most plausible cause for ordering the dust, that is, "combing" it in one direction.

## Electrical Currents in Space

We are thus led to believe that there may be magnetic fields in the spaces between the stars. But where can these magnetic fields originate? Even if stars are magnetic as, indeed, we know some stars to be, their field cannot extend far into space. This is just as on the earth. Although we have a magnetic field that is strong enough to align the navigator's compass needle, yet if one went out as far as the moon there would be virtually none of this magnetic field left. We must, therefore, look for the origin of this field not in the stars but in interstellar space itself. What can cause magnetic fields there? The only reasonable cause we can imagine is electric currents. And, indeed, it does not seem at all farfetched to believe that electric currents may be circulating through the vast spaces between the stars. For although a thick gas like air is a good insulator, a very tenuous gas like the material filling the space between the stars that has been irradiated with light is a material that can be shown to be a splendid conductor of electricity. Virtually no effort is needed to keep a current going in such material once it has started. We are, therefore, not surprised that such currents may persist in this material for enormous lengths of time producing magnetic fields whose consequences we can observe in the polarization of starlight. What originally caused the magnetic fields is, of course, quite a different question, and one to which there is not yet any very clear answer in sight.

From the few indications that the astronomer has, he can therefore say a good deal about conditions in the space between the stars. He knows that there are large clouds of dust and that there is gas which may be widely distributed, and partly also condensed into clouds. He can say a little bit about the chemical composition of the clouds of dust and gas. And he has been able to infer the existence of magnetic fields in these enormous regions. Yet another way in which they can be explored is by radio astronomy. It has turned out that hydrogen gas, one of the most difficult to observe optically, though probably by far the most common in the space between the stars, emits radio waves of a very particular frequency. They can be observed on the earth, and they give us a wealth of information, previously unobtainable by optical means, about the distribution of hydrogen gas in the spaces between the stars. In these ways we have come to know that there are swirling clouds of gas and dust in space whose motion and behavior are of the utmost importance for the stars themselves, although the gas and dust are far less easy to observe than the stars which are such a prominent feature of our night sky.

# VIII. The Earth's Radiation Belts

One of the most beautiful natural spectacles on the earth is the Aurora. In certain regions of the earth almost every night there is a marvelous show of tremendous waving luminous bands high in the atmosphere, sometimes red, sometimes blue, a spectacle of grandeur and beauty. It is seldom seen in England and is observed at its best in Canada and Alaska. On occasions, however, the Aurora is visible from far wider regions. There have

FIG. 30.  *There is a close connection between the frequency of sunspots and the occurrence of polar lights, which are caused by streams of charged particles emitted into space by the sun. On nearing the earth they are affected by the earth's magnetic field and reach the upper atmosphere in the polar zones, where they cause the phenomenon known as Aurora Borealis (in the north) and Aurora Australis (in the south).*

been occasions in England when the northern sky has appeared to be of luminous red color. So unexpected and powerful has this been that on such nights false calls to the fire brigade are no rarity, for people really believe that this glow must come from a fire in the vicinity. There have been occasions when the Aurora has been seen even as far south as the Mediterranean.

## The Aurora

What is the Aurora, and why does it occur in the main just in these very special regions? It is best to look first at the geographical distribution. This is seen to be asso-

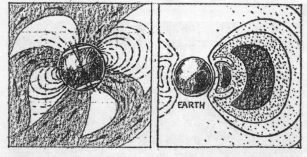

FIG. 31. *Some think the Aurora may originate in the effect charged particles from the sun have on molecules in our atmosphere. Charged particles deflected in the earth's magnetic field enter the polar light zones and cause the molecules to emit light. The white bands show the region where Aurora occurs. The radiation belts around the earth are represented at the right in terms of the concentration of particles occurring in different regions. The dark regions indicate a relatively high concentration of particles and the light regions relatively few particles.*

ciated with the earth's magnetism. As we all know, the earth acts as a magnet, a very useful property indeed, for it enables the mariner to find north by the use of a simple magnetic compass, as was first discovered by the Chinese long ago. Unfortunately, however, the direction indicated by the magnetic needle does not point exactly to the North Pole. Not only are there local deviations that may, for example, be due to large deposits of iron, but the magnetic pole of the earth, as it is called, is not where the geographic North Pole is. The magnetic pole of the earth is just north of Prince of Wales Island, Canada. If now one looks where the Aurora is seen most often, then it turns out that this is in a belt of places all around 1500 miles from the magnetic North Pole. As this pole is in Canada, the belt, where the Aurora is seen most frequently, dips farthest south in that country. In Canada and Alaska and, to some extent, in Iceland, the Auroral Zone passes through populated country. There is also a Southern Auroral Zone, which similarly forms a belt round the Southern Magnetic Pole, which itself lies in Antarctica. This zone does not cross any populous countries, nor any routes where ships or aircraft commonly pass. Thus the Southern Aurora has not been seen by so many people as the Northern one, although it, too, has been studied closely by scientists. It is then clear that the Aurora must have some connection with the earth's magnetism.

The Aurora is so high up that the atmosphere there is exceedingly thin, but something makes it glow, and this something was soon suspected to be fast-moving particles that come from outside the earth. Evidently, the motion of these particles is affected by the earth's magnetic field. Therefore, the particles are electrically charged. A great deal of work has been done by many scientists trying to find out more about these mysterious particles that come in from outer space, and provide this beautiful illumination high up in the atmosphere. Before long, people could connect it with disturbances in the earth's magnetic field that were also suspected to be due to particles coming in from far away. These same particles also influence the propagation of radio waves, and so the reception of radio messages. Next, it turned out that all these phenomena were connected with sunspots, this well-known rash that appears on the surface of the sun and fades again and appears again in eleven-year cycles.

## Trapped Particles

Though much thought was given to these interesting phenomena, entirely new light was thrown on the whole subject in the last few years by observations made by

FIG. 32. *Charged particles oscillate continuously in space from pole to pole. Recently rockets have detected the trapped particles and shown that they follow the path of the earth's magnetic field. The spiral path of a particle along a magnetic line of force from pole to pole is shown here. There are countless millions of them.*

instruments in high-flying rockets and artificial satellites. For, by these means, instruments were taken far higher than the region where the Aurora occurs. The early Russian satellites, although they carried massive instruments, did not go quite high enough to observe these astonishing phenomena in much detail; but the American lunar probes that went far into outer space and then returned again through the upper atmosphere of the earth gave much information. It turned out that about 10,000 miles above the surface of the earth there was an enormous amount of trapped radiation; far more charged particles crowded these regions than expected. These zones are enormous in extent. The bigger one is at its highest (10,000 miles up) above the earth's equator and dips down a little toward the magnetic poles of the earth. There, the extreme edge of this belt of particles dips low enough to touch the outer atmosphere of the earth, and there the flow of particles makes the atmosphere glow, thus producing the Aurora.

The second, smaller zone of radiation is confined to the equatorial regions of the earth and is around 2000 miles above the surface. We may picture these belts of radiation as cages for charged particles. The bars of the cage are provided by the magnetic field of the earth. This forms something like a trap; a cloud of charged particles, one of those that give rise to interruption of radio communications and to disturbances of the compass, goes into this cage but finds it very hard to leave it. Up there the particles are constrained to follow the lines of the magnetic field; they rush first north, then south, in a curious corkscrew motion, going forward and backward, and backward and forward; they just continue to exist up there, for there is nothing that interferes with them. Only a very small proportion of all these particles go far enough down to collide with the molecules of the earth's outermost atmosphere and thus end their career in the radiation belts. The result of these collisions is the glow of the Aurora. What we can see then in the Aurora is only a tiny part of the radiation that is there. It is rather like an iceberg, nine tenths of whose mass lies under the surface of the sea. Far more than nine tenths of the radiation lies well above the atmosphere and so does not become visible as the auroral glow. Probably most of these particles originate in the sun in special outbursts that are connected with sunspots.

No doubt these radiation belts are inconvenient for the space traveler. If one really wants to get right away from the earth to the moon or beyond, one has to pass through this belt of radiation. Unless one is very well shielded, the radiation would be an extreme hazard to health. Shielding means weight, and weight is a very expensive item for the space traveler. Weight limitations are going to be much more severe, I am sure, than in air travel. Though these radiation belts may be an obstacle to our ambitions in the space-travel field, they are of great and encouraging interest in quite another and probably more useful human endeavor, the attempt to construct power stations working on the fusion principle. This is the fusion of hydrogen to make helium which, it will be remembered, is the source of the energy for the sun and most of the stars. In order to achieve the enormous production of power that could result from the use of very ordinary materials in this way, it is necessary to have very high temperatures, of the same order as in the centers of the stars. Thus, the question arises, not only how to create such enormous temperatures but how to contain them.

## Magnetic Bottles

At these temperatures naturally every material is a gas, and so a bottle is required to hold gas of exceedingly high temperatures such as can presumably be obtained by passing a sufficiently powerful electric current through the gas. No material could possibly stand up to these temperatures; but the proposal is to use a magnetic field to contain the gas, just as in the radiation belts round the earth the particles are bottled up by a magnetic field. A magnetic bottle would seem to be the only solution to this problem, but whether it is a possible solution or not nobody at present knows. A tremendous amount of work is going on to solve this question for, in this direction, lies the cheapest, as well as the safest, source of power that one can imagine.

A fusion-power generating station would have two great advantages over the fission-type atomic-power station such as the existing one at Calder Hall and the many now being built throughout Britain, the United States, the U.S.S.R., France, and other countries. First, the raw material is very much cheaper; instead of uranium one would use hydrogen, which, after all, in the form of water is an exceedingly common commodity. Probably, the heavy variant of hydrogen would be required, but even this is in much more abundant supply than uranium. More important still, the core of a fission-type power station is bound to produce highly radioactive ash which it will be increasingly difficult and expensive to dispose of. In a fusion-type power station, if this could in fact be built, there would be no radioactive ash. The very simple materials that go into it all lead to perfectly stable end products having no radioactivity. However, the provision of a suitable magnetic bottle seems to be extremely difficult; in spite of the tremendous efforts put into various experimental fusion devices, no solution to the problem has yet emerged. One is reminded in this connection of one of the problems the medieval alchemists faced. One of their objects, in addition to making gold, was to find a universal solvent—a fluid that would dissolve every material that came into contact with it. But before they could get anywhere with making this fluid, they faced the absurd problem of how, if they ever made it, they could contain it. What bottle could hold a fluid that would dissolve everything? This is the problem the research workers in the fusion field face, and the only conceivable solution, the magnetic bottle, has not yet been demonstrated to be possible except perhaps in the radiation belts of the earth.

## Magnetism in Space

The earth is by no means the only magnetic body in space. The sun, too, has a general magnetic field of about the same strength as the earth's, but in addition there are also highly localized but very much stronger magnetic fields associated with the sunspots. It is a little surprising that a body so very much larger than the earth, as the sun is, should have a magnetic field no stronger than that of the earth. Some stars are observed to have very strong magnetic fields, thousands of times stronger than that of the earth. More puzzling still, the direction of the magnetic field of some of these stars seems to change every few hours. How such an enormous magnet can be switched round in such a short period is something which, so far, completely baffles all our attempts to find an explanation.

Before the coming of the electric motor, less than a century ago, the only use of magnetism on the earth was as the mariner's compass and for the purpose of toys. Now, of course, we produce magnetic fields in all sorts of machinery, notably all electric generators and motors, but natural magnetic fields on the earth are rather weak and do not seem to be of great importance. Apparently in space the reverse is true. It seems more and more as though, once we go away from the earth, magnetism increases enormously in importance. In our vicinity this is shown by the radiation belts I have just described. Farther away magnetic stars and especially the interstellar magnetic fields described in the previous chapter are a dominant force. We will not be able to understand the construction of the galaxies fully until we have mastered the understanding of the magnetic fields in outer space.

# IX. The Law of Gravitation

Nearly three hundred years ago Sir Isaac Newton formulated the Law of Gravitation. With it, the first of the great forces of nature was described in a useful and fertile way. In the familiar story it was the falling of an apple that suggested to Newton the possibility that the motion of the moon might be due to the same force as the motion of the apple. The magnitude of this step is not always appreciated. Newton attempted to find, and was successful in finding, the law that connects objects as vastly different in size and in distance from the earth as the apple and the moon. The moon, 250,000 miles away, is maybe one hundred million times farther from the surface of the earth than the apple was when it began to fall; and the diameter of the moon bears to the diameter of the apple a ratio nearly as great. When a scientist proposes a law of nature, then it is always his aim to describe as many different natural events as possible; but it was bold indeed to suggest that two events as different as the motion of the moon and the motion of the apple could be comprehended in one law. However, not only does the law bridge this gap, but we know that its validity extends further on either side. In addition to the motion of the moon round the earth, the motion of the planets round the sun is described by it—a step of a thousand or so in size. But beyond this the motions of binary stars, the motions of stars in the galaxy, indeed, presumably, the motions of galaxies in a cluster of galaxies are governed by the same law that controls the motion of the apple. In this final example, the distances between the galaxies are a million million times as great as the distance between the moon and the earth. Newton's Law of Gravitation, therefore, covers an enormous range of sizes, greater indeed than we know for certain for any other law of nature.

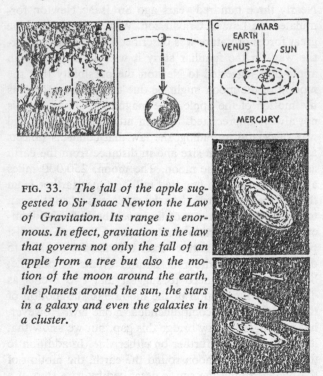

FIG. 33. *The fall of the apple suggested to Sir Isaac Newton the Law of Gravitation. Its range is enormous. In effect, gravitation is the law that governs not only the fall of an apple from a tree but also the motion of the moon around the earth, the planets around the sun, the stars in a galaxy and even the galaxies in a cluster.*

## Inverse Square Law

When Newton had decided to examine the possibility that the motion of the moon was due to the gravitational pull of the earth just as much as the fall of the apple was, he still had to decide on how the strength of this pull varied with distance from the earth. What he proposed has become known as the inverse square law. This says that the gravitational attraction of a body varies with the inverse square of the distance. In other words, if you double the distance you diminish the strength of the attraction to a quarter of what it previously was.

FIG. 34. *The Attractive Force Produced by a Sphere. The sum of the attractive forces had to be worked out and evaluated. Newton found that if a body is spherical (as the earth almost is), then the attraction of the whole sphere on any particle (see left) inside or outside the earth is the same as if the whole mass were concentrated in the center. This remarkable property is not shared by any other law of force. A person on the earth x (see right) is attracted by all the many particles that make up the earth. Each pulls in its own direction but the pulls combine to direct the force of gravity toward the center of the earth. If, however, this pull of gravitation suddenly ceased, the person would fly off into space.*

This law has many interesting properties which are of great help to the mathematician when he tries to work out its consequences. The first of these was discovered by Newton by mathematical methods that were quite recondite for the age. He faced the question that if each particle of the earth attracted the apple (and, of course, the moon), then the sum of all these attractions had to be evaluated before one could work out how fast the apple (or the moon) would fall. These attractions differ both in magnitude (owing to the greatly different distances between different particles of the earth and the apple) and in direction. How are they all to be added up? In fact, such an addition can be a very difficult calculation; but fortunately the earth is almost spherical in shape. If it is assumed to have complete spherical symmetry, then, as Newton found, the attraction of the whole earth on any particle outside the earth is the same as if its whole mass were concentrated at its center. This is a remarkably simple result—one that is not shared by any other law of force. Another remarkable result, closely connected with this one, concerns the field inside a spherical shell of matter.

Imagine the space between two concentric spheres to be filled uniformly with matter. What is the attraction of this matter at an interior point? If we consider a particle in the interior but not at the center, then clearly by symmetry the attraction must lie along the diameter through the particle. It could be either toward the part of the shell nearest to the particle, or in the opposite direction. The part of the shell nearest the particle has less mass, but is closer to it than the part farther away. Which of these two opposing influences will win? It turns out that, with the inverse square law of force, and with that law alone, there is no attraction whatever inside the shell. If the force depended more strongly on distance, then the particle would be attracted to the part of the shell nearest it; if it depended less strongly on distance, it would be attracted to the opposite side, that is, toward the center. The inverse square law falls exactly between these two possibilities—there is no force whatever. From these properties of the inverse square law one can deduce another one.

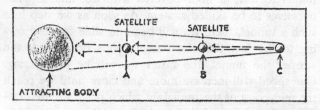

FIG. 35.  *When Newton examined the possibility that the motion of the moon was due to the gravitational pull of the earth, he still had to determine how the pull varied with distance. The result which he obtained became known as the inverse square law. At A there is a certain force between the satellite and the attracting body, but when the same satellite is twice as far away, at B, it experiences only one quarter of the force it did at A. At three times the distance (C), the force is reduced to one ninth of that at A.*

## Tunnels through the Earth

We shall suppose that the earth is exactly spherical and uniform in composition. Then, if tunneling were cheap and easy, one might think of the following way of getting from any point on the surface of the earth to any other: one would make a straight tunnel in the direct line between the two points. If the two places are relatively near, then the mouths of the tunnel will be gently inclined; if the two places are far apart, they will be steeply inclined; and if one wishes to connect a place with its antipodes, the tunnel would be vertical and go straight through the center of the earth. Next, let us suppose that we use a very good lubricant so that we can slide freely through any such tunnel without any friction whatever. We may suppose, for example, the tunnel to have a floor covered with ice, and suppose ourselves to be skilled skaters. As soon as we step into such a tunnel, then, we will begin to slide forward owing to the fact that the tunnel points downward; the steeper the tunnel, the faster we will be progressing. Our speed will increase more and more until we reach the mid-point of the tunnel, at which place we are closest to the center of the earth. From there on, we begin to get nearer to the surface, that is, we begin to

FIG. 36. *An interesting property of the inverse square law is the fact that the angle of descent governs speed and also the distance covered. Thus, if it were possible to bore a series of straight tunnels through the earth to places at different distances, the tunnels would differ in inclination according to their geographical position. Travelers could then reach these places by simply sliding down them. A long tunnel, being steep, would be traversed at high speed; a shorter, and therefore more gently inclined tunnel, would lead to a journey at low speed. In fact, the same time would be taken by each such journey, namely, 42 minutes.*

climb, although the direction of the tunnel remains the same. Thus our speed will diminish and, in fact, we will come to a standstill the moment we reach our destination.

How long does this journey take? If we want to go to a place not very far away, we have no great distance to cover; but, on the other hand, our tunnel is at such a gentle inclination that we do not move very fast. If we want to go to a very distant place, we have to cover a long distance but we start off with a very high acceleration. It turns out that, once again, these two influences cancel. Wherever we wish to go by this method, it will take us exactly the same time, *namely, 42 minutes*. Not, perhaps, a very high speed, if we only want to go to a place a mile away; but a very fast means of travel if we want to go to the far side of the earth. In fact, of course, not only is tunneling extremely expensive, and frictionless sliding not a technical possibility, but the earth is not quite uniform. The central regions are considerably denser than the outer ones. If we contemplate tunneling through such a non-uniform earth, then it would make travel to very distant places faster by a few minutes than in the case of the uniform earth without, however, affecting the travel time to nearer localities.

### Weightlessness

One of the most remarkable properties of gravitation was discovered by Galileo before Newton's time: the fact that all bodies fall equally fast. It is this universal nature of gravitation which distinguishes it most markedly from all other forces. There is no way of escaping from gravitation, though many writers of science fiction from its earliest beginnings have contemplated this possibility. To the best of our knowledge Galileo's rule is exactly true—all bodies without exception fall equally fast. Free falling is an experience few of us have; however, we can attempt to imagine what this would feel like. Suppose we were in a box which was falling freely. Then we ourselves and all the objects around us would be pursuing the same motion since all bodies fall equally fast. Inside this box, therefore, gravitation would not exist. It would have been abolished by the free fall. We could not pour water out of a glass since the water wouldn't know which way to go, there being no gravita-

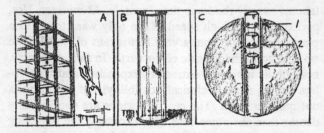

FIG. 37. *One of the most remarkable properties of gravitation is the fact that all bodies fall equally fast. For instance, if a workman falls from a building under construction (A), he falls at the same speed as the tools he was handling when he slipped. This property distinguishes gravitation from all other forces. To establish this property of gravitation with precision, air resistance has to be eliminated by the use of a vacuum tube. In such a tube a steel ball and a feather dropped together (B) will reach the bottom simultaneously. In a long free fall (C) particles tend to draw together. Consider a box containing two particles in it. Assume the box commences to fall down a tunnel through the center of the earth. As the box falls, the particles come closer together and finally collide at the center of attraction (3).*

tion. We could, though, pull the glass away from the water and leave the water behind as a floating blob. We ourselves would be floating weightlessly, and the whole situation would be most remarkable. This situation is, in fact, what must be contemplated in connection with space flight. Once the rocket motors of the spaceship have been switched off, the whole spaceship and its inhabitants fall freely. Thus they have to get used to traveling in this state of weightlessness. Many problems of a medical and physical character arise that have to be considered, and are being considered at the present time. To mention but one of them: there is danger of suffocation in one's sleep. Normally, the exhaled air is warmer than the surrounding air and so will be lighter and thus will rise away from the breathing person. He will have fresh air to breathe in. However, in a condition of weightlessness the relative lightness of the exhaled air would not impart any motion to it, for it would not know in what direction to "rise", there being no gravity. Thus, without extensive provision of fans people would tend (particularly in their sleep) to breathe in the air they had just exhaled, with disastrous consequences. The whole situation is so different from anything we know that a great deal of thought will have to be spent before the problems can be solved satisfactorily.

## Einstein's Gravity

The universal nature of gravitation forms the very basis of the successor to Newton's theory of gravitation, namely, Einstein's celebrated General Theory of Relativity. Whereas the fact that all bodies fall equally fast is only a more or less incidental point in Newton's theory, it forms the very basis of Einstein's theory. In the first instance, Einstein suggests that our normal state is rather exceptional and possibly not the most fruitful one to consider. By our normal state our existence on earth is meant, where we feel gravity all the time and are virtually never in a state of free fall. This condition is only made possible by the solidity of the earth. We sit or stand or lie on solid objects that themselves are supported by structures, such as houses on the solid earth, which stand up to gravitation. We thus should consider our weight not so much as a consequence of gravitation, as of the fact that we happen to rest on a solid surface supporting ourselves against the gravitational pull. He observes that, if there were no gravitation but we were in a spaceship with its rocket motors working full blast, accelerating it all the time, the conditions inside that spaceship would be very much like conditions we are accustomed to, for every object has inertia, which means that a force must be exerted on it to accelerate it. Thus, in the accelerating spaceship, objects have weight and they all fall equally fast if their support is withdrawn.

Where, then, does the true nature of gravitation show itself? Consider, again, the freely falling box, falling through a shaft passing from the surface of the earth through its center. Inside this box there will be conditions of weightlessness; but, as Einstein points out, if we examine conditions there very, very closely, then we will indeed find some evidence of the earth's gravitation. Consider two particles that were at rest on opposite sides of the box before the box started to fall. They are each falling freely toward the center of the earth. Therefore, by the time the box passes through the center of the earth these two particles will collide in the box. Thus there is a tiny bit of gravitation that we cannot abolish by living in a freely falling box, which makes two particles originally at rest on opposite walls collide while the box covers the radius of the earth. From this consideration Einstein constructs his new theory of gravitation. Almost all its results are identical with those of Newton's theory; but there are a few very small effects which are different. The observational tests favor Einstein's theory and speak against Newton's. However, Einstein's theory of gravitation is mathematically most cumbersome. We know that it gives the same answer as Newton's to any practical problem other than one or two exceedingly refined ones. Therefore, in practice, we continue to use Newton's theory for all but these very small points, because it is simpler to handle and gives the same results as Einstein's, results that are in excellent agreement with observation.

# X. The Motion of Celestial Bodies

The consequences of the law of gravitation are most readily studied in space. There gravitation appears in a simpler form than anywhere else. On the earth we know that various other forces always intervene and make it difficult to study gravitation in isolation. Thus the resistance of air to motion causes light objects, like leaves, to fall much more slowly than heavy objects like stones. For many centuries this obscured the law discovered by Galileo that, in the absence of other forces such as the resistance of air, all bodies do in fact fall equally fast. Again, for example, when the structure of stars is considered, gravitation undoubtedly is of the utmost importance. But other forces, such as gas pressure and the effects of radiation, have to be considered before any conclusions can be reached about the structure of the stars. It is only when we study the motion of bodies such as planets and satellites that we can be reasonably certain that no force other than gravitation is of much significance.

## The Sun's Force

What, then, does Newton's Law of Gravitation say about the motion of celestial bodies? First, as has been said already, the attraction of a spherical body is the same as that of a particle of the same mass at the center of the sphere. If a body is not spherical, then the attraction outside is somewhat different; but the difference

111

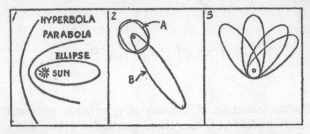

FIG. 38. *The law of gravitation is most easily studied in space. On the earth many other forces intervene, such as air resistance, friction, etc. Gas pressure and radiation must be taken into account when considering the structure of stars. But when we study the motion of such bodies as planets and satellites, we become reasonably certain that gravitation is of paramount importance. (1) Thus we find that the huge size of the sun compared with that of the planets causes these planets and other bodies to orbit in conic section; that is, in ellipses, parabolas or hyperbolas. A body in an ellipse retraces its path again and again. Bodies in parabolic or hyperbolic orbits approach the sun only once. (2) Most planets move in circles or nearly circular ellipses. Many comets move in highly elongated ellipses. Planetary orbits have shapes such as A. Cometary orbits have shapes such as B. (3) According to general relativity the elliptical orbits do not close completely and so rotate slowly. The effect of this rotation of the long axis of the ellipse is greatly exaggerated in this drawing. In the case of a fast-moving planet, such as Mercury, the ellipse is turned right around after twelve million orbits.*

between the actual attraction and that of the spherical body of the same mass diminishes rapidly as we go away from the body. The planets are so nearly spherical, and the distances between them are so large compared with their diameters, that we can treat them as particles. Furthermore, calculations are greatly simplified by the fact that the mass of the sun vastly exceeds the mass of any of the planets. Thus, though the different planets attract each other, the motion of each planet is in the main due to the sun alone, and the other planets cause only minor deviations from this. The motion of a particle in the field of attraction of a massive body is easily shown to be a conic section—that is, an ellipse, a parabola, or a hyperbola, with the massive body at the focus. The ellipse is by far the most important of these, for it alone leads to a recurrence. A particle in a parabolic or hyperbolic path comes but once and then goes away forever. Ellipses can be of many different shapes. They can be circular, or they may have very elongated shapes. It turns out that the planets in general follow very nearly circular orbits, ellipses that differ only by a little from a circle.

If we want to consider the motion of planets not only under the influence of the sun but also of each other, a problem of very great mathematical complexity is reached. The simplest of these, when we consider only two planets and the sun, leads to the celebrated problem of three bodies on which an enormous amount of mathematical ingenuity has been spent. It is clear that, in the general case when the three bodies have more or less equal masses, orbits of tremendous variety and complexity can arise; but no complete understanding of this problem has been reached. Fortunately, this is not necessary in order to find the motion of the planets owing to the overwhelming mass of the sun, which exceeds that of Jupiter, the next heaviest body, by a factor of a thousand. In the difficult subject of celestial mechanics, one therefore starts from the simple elliptical orbits and then considers the minor deviations from these ellipses that are due to the other planets. Nevertheless, the discussion is of great mathematical complexity and length. Nowadays, modern electronic calculating machines are employed more and more to solve the problems arising.

At this point, one of the major differences between Newton's and Einstein's theories of gravitation may be mentioned. If only the sun and one planet are considered, Newton's theory leads to an ellipse; but Einstein's theory does not lead quite to an ellipse. In each revolution the orbit is virtually the same as an ellipse; but the figure does not quite close; so that, over long periods, the ellipse is actually rotating about the sun. This effect had been noted in the case of the innermost planet, Mercury, well before the formulation of Einstein's theory of relativity. Since then, this relativistic effect has also been confirmed in the orbits of several other planets. This motion of the major axis of the ellipses of the planetary orbits is one of the main observational results that support Einstein's theory of gravitation rather than Newton's.

## The Orbits of Satellites

Comets are also members of the solar system. They, too, move in elliptic orbits; but theirs are mostly very far from circular. In particular, in the case of the so-called long-period comets, the ellipses are very greatly elongated. Next, consider the motion of satellites. A somewhat different problem arises here. The moons of the various planets, including our own, are often so close to the planet itself that the orbit is affected by the planet's shape differing from a sphere. Thus, the motion of the moon about the earth is not a simple ellipse (although it is rather close to one) but an extremely complicated

FIG. 39.  *If the earth were a perfect sphere, the satellite would follow a fixed ellipse. The earth, however, has a slight bulge at the equator. This causes the course of the satellite to be more complicated. The rings, such a distinctive feature of the planet Saturn, may be the debris of satellites that have been destroyed by the gravitational pull of the planet.*

figure whose evaluation requires the most recondite form of mathematics. Owing, presumably, to the rotation of the earth and the resulting centrifugal force, the earth is a somewhat flattened sphere. It has a bulge round its equator. At first sight, this would not seem to be significant, the difference in the polar and equatorial diameters of the earth being only a fraction of 1 per cent. Nevertheless, it has some effect on the motion of the moon, and is of tremendous importance for the motion of artificial satellites. If, for example, an orbit like that of the first Sputnik is considered, allowance must immediately be made for the figure of the earth. If the earth were a sphere, then such a satellite would move in an elliptical orbit around the earth, and the plane of this orbit would be irrelevant. It would not matter whether the satellite circled about the equator of the earth, or went from North Pole to equator, or to South Pole and

115

back, or along any intermediate inclination. Sputnik I, in fact, followed an orbit that took it up to 60 degrees North and 60 degrees South. On such an orbit the effect of the earth's equatorial bulge is particularly marked. It causes the entire ellipse to rotate about the earth. Thus the orbit of the satellite will not be a fixed curve among the stars of the night sky but will gradually sweep across a whole band of the celestial sphere.

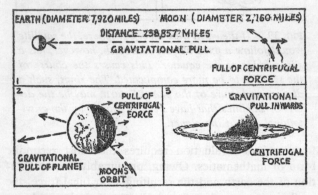

FIG. 40. *Why the Moon Always Shows the Same Side to the Earth. The moon is subject to the gravitational pull of the earth and to the centrifugal force of its own motion. The interplay of two such large forces stretches a body like the moon and eventually makes it rotate in such a way that it always shows the same face to the earth. As the moon moves in its orbit around the earth, the side farthest away from us moves faster (as it has farther to go) than the inner side (visible to us) and so the outer side experiences greater centrifugal force. If a satellite (such as the moon) came too close to its planet, the gravitational pull of the planet would cause the satellite to become distorted and break up. The resultant debris would produce a ring of small particles around the planet.*

116

In fact, the argument can be reversed. The exact figure of the earth is not easy to determine from the surface. Moreover, it does not tell us exactly what the earth's gravitational field is like because this depends also on the distribution of density with depth. However, from studying the motion of artificial satellites, and in particular the Sputnik and Vanguard satellites, it has become possible to find out much more about the figure of the earth and the variation of density with location than has ever been known before. When one considers a natural satellite, one must allow for the fact that not only the planet but the satellite, too, forms an extended body and not a particle. Since the part of the satellite nearest the planet will experience the greatest attractive force, whereas the part farthest from the planet moves with the greatest speed in the orbit and so has the greatest centrifugal force, great strains and stresses are set up within a moon. In the case of our own moon, these strains and stresses have eventually led to the well-known fact that the moon always shows the same face to the earth. There is a slight wobble in the motion of the moon, as a result of which about four sevenths of the surface of the moon have been known for a long time. The recent spectacular feat of Lunik III in photographing the far side of the moon was justly celebrated as a great scientific achievement.

If a moon came very close to a parent planet the strains and stresses set up in it might be so tremendous as to cause it to break up, and to form a cloud of dust. This is what has apparently happened to one or more moons of Saturn, and one presumes that the famous rings of Saturn have been formed in this way. In the course of time, the dust particles would collide with each other and eventually this would make them go into circular orbits and so finally they would surround the planet completely in one plane. However, they would be disturbed in their motions by the other satellites, of which Saturn in fact has a respectable number. It turns out that the existence of other satellites would lead to forbidden lanes in which none of the dusty remains of the innermost satellite could orbit. In this way, we can account for the divisions between the rings of Saturn, the dark lanes that separate the circular rings.

## The Speed of Meteors

Shooting stars, or meteors, are a familiar phenomenon. They form a fine spectacle and, in recent years, have been studied more and more both by optical and by radio means. They are formed by particles that are usually quite small but enter the earth's atmosphere at high speed and rapidly burn up, giving the well-known appearance of a fireball. Some swarms of meteors are periodic and recur every year. Others are sporadic. The recurring meteors clearly are members of our own solar system. They have orbits around the sun that bring a group of them into the earth's atmosphere whenever the earth happens to be in its own motion about the sun at the right place. With sporadic meteors the situation is not quite so obvious. They may be members of the solar system or they may come from farther directions. Most of the members of the solar system (though by no means the long period comets) move in the plane of the ecliptic, or near it. It has been shown by patient observation that most, if not all, meteors also move more or less within this plane, which strongly indicates that they are members of our solar system. Another test concerns their velocities. If they are in elliptic orbits, their velocities cannot be greater than 26 miles per second. Even should they be moving directly opposed to the velocity of the earth in its orbit (which is 19 miles per second) the apparent velocity cannot exceed 45 miles per second. On the other hand, if they came from outer space, their velocity would be bound to exceed 26 miles per second in their hyperbolic or parabolic orbits, and so a question of great interest is whether there are meteors whose velocity relative to the earth exceeds 45 miles per second. The indications are now pretty strong that there are no, or at most exceedingly few, such meteors. We have apparently no such visitors from outer space in our solar system.

## Gravity and Light

Another problem of gravitational orbits concerns the motion of light. In our ordinary experience we regard light as something without mass; but in the more refined language of modern physics this statement is of doubtful validity. The question, therefore, arises of whether light, too, falls in a gravitational field just as

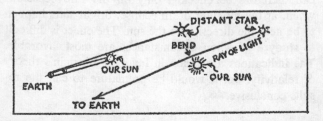

FIG. 41. *Einstein found that in the vicinity of the sun a ray of light from a distant star should be slightly bent. We can observe the bending only when the moon eclipses the sun.*

material objects fall. Newton's theory gives no unambiguous answer to this. In it, either light is not affected at all by gravitation, or it may be affected, though to only a certain extent which is very small indeed. Einstein's theory gives an unequivocal answer to the question—light does fall. However, as it moves so very fast, it falls but very little. This falling of light should become most marked in light coming very close to a very massive body. In our vicinity, this means a light ray going closely past the sun. According to Einstein's theory, a light ray just touching the sun's surface should be deflected by the sun's gravitational field through a small angle (a little less than two seconds of arc). According to Newton's theory the effect should be at most half that. It is an exceedingly difficult thing to observe such a minute deflection of a light ray. The only way we can hope to see it is by looking at stars past the sun, which is impossible in ordinary daylight. We must wait for an eclipse of the sun by the moon before there is any hope of observing this effect. Even during an eclipse it does not get very dark. Accordingly, it is impossible to see any but rather bright stars. Einstein's prediction can therefore be checked only on the rare occasions when, at the moment of an eclipse, bright stars happen to be near the direction to the sun. The effect is difficult to study even when circumstances are most favorable. The indications are much in favor of Einstein's theory of relativity, but it would be premature to call the results conclusive.

PLATE IX.    *Even today we can see the remains of a vast
explosion that was observed in* A.D. *1054 in the vast cloud
of luminous gas known as the Crab Nebula in* Taurus.

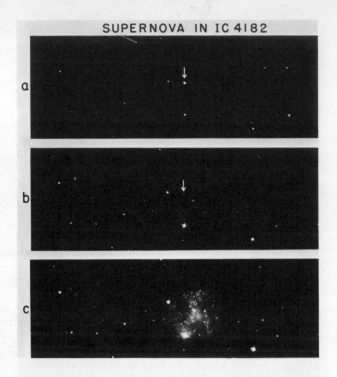

SUPERNOVA IN IC 4182

a

b

c

PLATE X. *A bright new star appears and fades away. In a nearby galaxy a new, very bright star appeared suddenly. The top photograph (1937) shows it at an early stage. It was so bright that only a very short exposure (20 min.) was required and therefore few other stars are shown. The middle photograph (1938) is much fainter in spite of doubling of the exposure (45 min.). The bottom photograph (1942), taken with a further doubling of exposure (85 min.), reveals no trace of the star, although with a longer exposure much other background detail is shown.*

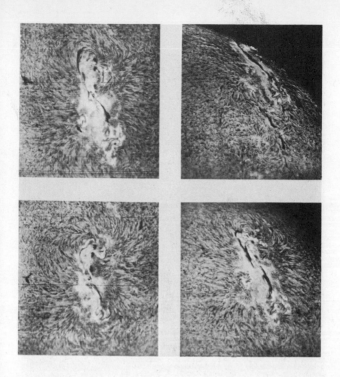

PLATE XI. *In these photographs of the southwest quarter of the sun—taken in August 1915 at intervals of two days—the bubbling of the surface layers is clearly visible.*

PLATE XII.    *The Owl Nebula in* Ursa Major *is a spherical
mass of gas shining mainly in the light of the central star.*

# XI. The Tides

Among the most remarkable side-effects of gravitation are the tides of the ocean, which are so familiar to all of us. Although many people are aware that the moon has something to do with the tides, it is not quite obvious why there should be two tides a day when the moon only rises once a day. It requires rather a close analysis, already briefly indicated in the previous chapter, to show just how the tidal forces arise.

When two bodies such as, for example, the earth and the moon move under the influence of each other's gravitation, then they both move about the point that is known as the common center of mass. In order to find it, we draw a line joining the centers of the two bodies and divide it in the ratio of their masses. The point we so find is the common center of mass. If the two bodies have equal mass, then the common center of mass divides the line joining the centers evenly, and so is in the middle. If one body is much more massive than the other, then the common center of mass is much closer to the massive body. The earth being some 80 times more massive than the moon, the common center of mass is rather close to the center of the earth; in fact, it is still well inside the body of the earth. However, this does not affect the discussion.

## Forces between Double Stars

If we consider a double star, with two stars of equal mass moving about the common center of mass in circles, then we have about the simplest system one can imagine. The force of gravitation pulls the two stars together, centrifugal force keeps them apart. If we now look at one of these stars, we see that the *whole* star will be attracted by the other star, but the side nearest to the other star will be attracted most and the side farthest away will be attracted least, since gravitation falls off with distance by the inverse square law. Also, since the whole star is rushing about the common center of mass in its circular orbit, the entire star will feel the pull of centrifugal force. However, the part nearest the other star moves with the smallest speed and so experiences least centrifugal force; whereas, the part farthest from the other star moves at the highest speed and so it experiences the greatest centrifugal force. Thus, the side of the star nearest its neighbor has the maximum of gravitational pull and the minimum of centrifugal force, whereas the opposite is true on the other side.

On the average, over the whole star, centrifugal force and gravitation exactly balance. This is how the star stays in its orbit. But if the two forces balance when averaged

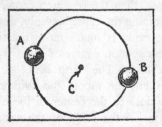

FIG. 42. *When two bodies of equal mass (A and B) orbit about each other, they describe the same circle. If unequal in mass, the larger describes a smaller circle than the other. The center of the circle, C, midway between A and B, remains at rest.*

over the whole star, then clearly on the side nearest the other star gravitation is greater than centrifugal force, whereas the opposite is true on the opposite side. Thus, on balance, there is a force toward the other star at the side nearest to it, and a force away from it on the side farthest from it. These forces, which are due to a local lack of balance between gravitation and centrifugal force, are called tide-raising forces. It will have been noticed that they are due to the difference in gravitation and centrifugal force across the star, not to the absolute value of either force. When one works out the details of this, it emerges that these tide-raising forces vary not like the inverse square but like the inverse cube of the distance.

### Sun Tides vs. Moon Tides

If we come now to the earth and the moon, then it follows that there is a force toward the moon on the side of the earth nearest the moon, and a force away from the moon on the side farthest from the moon. Thus, if the whole earth were covered by a uniform ocean, the water level would rise both on the side nearest the moon and on the opposite side, and be lower over the rest of the earth. One can work out by how much the sea would rise, and the result is the remarkably low figure of around 16 inches. However, the earth is gravitationally attracted not only by the moon but also—and much more importantly—by the sun. The sun is a vastly greater body than the moon and its mass is nearly 30 million times the mass of the moon. But it is nearly 400 times as far away from the earth as the moon. The tide-raising forces, as we have mentioned, vary with the inverse cube of the distance, and when we work through all these figures, then it turns out that the tidal effect of the sun is only half the effect of the moon. Thus, on a uniformly covered earth the ocean would rise about 8 inches as a result of the action of the sun as compared with 16 inches as a result of the action of the moon.

How do the tides of the sun and of the moon combine? Clearly, if the sun and the moon are in the same direction, then the high tides due to the two bodies will occur in the same places and so will add, the solar high tide, as it were, coming on top of the lunar one. If the sun and the moon are in opposite directions, then the tides will also add, for the high tide due to the sun on the side of the earth nearest the sun will occur at the same place as the high tide due to the moon on the side

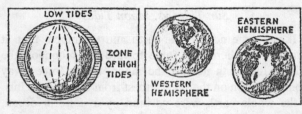

FIG. 43. *What would happen if the whole of the earth's surface were covered with water? Two large tidal bulges would project, one on the side nearest to the moon and one on the opposite side. On the right the side of the earth nearer the moon is the zone of high tides, while the opposite side of the earth also experiences a high tide because of the earth's rotation about the common center of gravity. The dash lines indicate the general region of low tides. These drawings of the western and eastern hemispheres of the earth show that the water that covers about three quarters of the planet's surface is restricted by land masses. This fact greatly modifies the tides.*

of the earth farthest from the moon. Thus whenever the sun and the moon are in the same or the opposite directions, the two tides will occur in the same places and will add, making a tide of 2 feet on a uniformly covered earth. When the moon is in the same direction as the sun, then we have a new moon, and when the moon is in the opposite direction from the sun, we have a full moon. Thus the tides add at new moon and at full moon, resulting in the so-called spring tides. However, when the moon is in first quarter or third quarter, then the sea is high due to the moon just where it is low due to the sun; and it is high due to the sun just where it is low due to the moon. Thus the tides will be very much smaller and are called neap tides.

## The Reason for Higher Tides

It is remarkably disappointing that the theory of the tides leads to a maximum rise of the ocean of only 2 feet, for we are all familiar with very much higher tides. However, these arise entirely out of the curious interaction of land and sea owing to the extraordinarily complicated coast lines that there are all round the earth. We know the tides only round the coast lines. It is exceedingly difficult to measure what the tides are in midocean. However, there is little reason to believe that they are very different from the maximum of 2 feet predicted by the simple theory. The tides rise particularly high if the coast line has such a shape that the rising water is channeled into a narrowing waterway. A particularly fine example of this is the Bay of Fundy, the part of the ocean between New Brunswick and Nova Scotia. Owing to its funnel shape the tides at the head of the bay have a range of well over 40 feet, the highest known in the

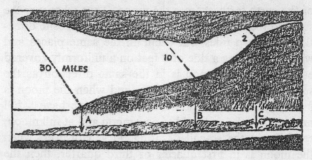

FIG. 44. *How the Tide Rises along a Narrowing Bay. Suppose at point A the bay is 30 miles wide and a body of water 5 feet high is moving inland. By the time this wave reaches point B, only one third as wide, the wave is 15 feet high, and if it were not for friction against the bottom of the bay, the tidal wave would continue to build up its height as it progressed up the bay. (The bottom part of the drawing is a cross-sectional view showing the contour of the bottom and the contour of the tidal wave.)*

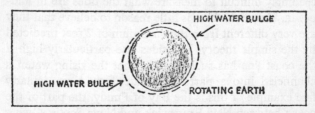

FIG. 45. *While the earth is turning, the moon holds the tidal bulges in position. Thus the rotating earth is continuously rubbing against the fixed tidal bulges.*

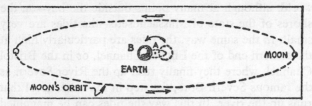

FIG. 46. *Why There Are Two Tides a Day. The earth not only attracts the moon, but also is attracted by the moon. Thus the earth, too, has to go around a circle which, since the earth is much more massive, is much smaller than that described by the moon. In this circular motion of the earth side B, being farther from the center of the circle, suffers the greatest centrifugal force, while side A, being nearer the moon, suffers the greatest attraction. The two forces are in balance at the center of the earth. This centrifugal force raises a tide at B and gravitation raises a tide at A.*

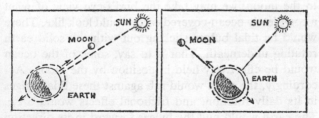

FIG. 47. *Spring tides (left) are caused by the sun and moon pulling together and thus producing a high tide. This happens when the moon is new and when it is full. Neap tides (right) are caused when the sun and the moon are at right angles to each other. In this case the high tide due to the moon's attraction is decreased by that of the sun. Thus the tidal range is diminished. This happens at the first and last quarters of the moon.*

127

world, although at many points outside the bay—on the shores of the state of Massachusetts—the tides are very small. In the same way, the tides are particularly high at the eastern end of the English Channel, or in the Bristol Channel, where they finally rush up the River Severn as the famous Severn Bore, the step in the water level that runs up the river. In this way the tides can be magnified enormously by a suitable shape of the coast line. On the other hand, if we have a relatively small landlocked sea, like the Baltic or the Black Sea, then since virtually the whole of it is at the same time at high water or low water, and not enough water can come through the narrow exits to raise or lower the water level, there are virtually no tides.

## Tidal Friction

An important effect of the tides is the so-called tidal friction. Concentrating for a moment on the tides due to the moon, we may take the bird's-eye view of what a completely ocean-covered earth would look like. There would be tidal bulges sticking out with the solid earth rotating underneath. That is to say, some of the ocean would be effectively held in position by the moon. Accordingly, the earth would rub against these tidal bulges in its daily rotation, and frictional effects would arise. The earth would pull the bulges forward in its direction of rotation, and the bulges would tend to slow down the rotation of the earth as a whole. If one works out what this comes to, not just for the lunar tide but for the solar one as well, finds that there is very little of this friction where the ocean is deep. In other words, water is a very good lubricant where it is deep. It is only where the sea is fairly shallow that much tidal friction can arise. But, again, if the sea is shallow and landlocked like, say, the Baltic, then, since there are no tides, there will be no tidal friction. There are, however, some stretches of ocean, such as the Irish Sea, that have large tides and are fairly shallow, and it is these regions that produce most of the tidal friction. The tidal friction has two effects of importance. One is that since the bulges are pulled forward in the sense of the earth's rotation, they tend to accelerate the moon in its orbit and, in the course of time, they drive the moon a little farther away from the earth. In other words, the tidal bulges, pulled forward by the rotation of the earth, tend to communicate some of the rotation of the earth to the motion of the moon in its orbit. Secondly, it is clear that this tidal friction will tend to slow down the rotation of the earth, and a quick calculation will show that, in the past few billion years, the tides of the ocean will have supplied enough friction to change the time of the rotation of the earth about its axis from around eight hours to the present twenty-four.

## Atmospheric Tides

The tides of the ocean are not the only effect of the tide-raising forces. The solid earth itself gives a little, though only a very little, under the strains and stresses of the tidal forces; and in recent years it has become possible to measure the deformation of the solid earth due to the tides. Much greater is the effect of the tidal forces on the earth's atmosphere. Clearly, the mantle of air surrounding the earth can be looked upon as another sort of ocean, and, just like the seas, we could expect it to rise and fall with the tide. As the atmosphere covers the earth uniformly, we could expect a much simpler situation than in the case of the ocean that beats upon so

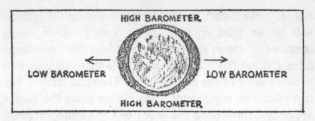

FIG. 48. *The sun and the moon also produce tides in our atmosphere, drawing it out in opposite directions precisely as they do with water.*

many shores. On the other hand, it is easy to watch the surface of the ocean, but it is much harder to notice what the top of the atmosphere does (or, at least, *was* much harder before the United States launched the Tiros I weather satellite). The only way in which we can conveniently study the behavior of the top of the atmosphere is by watching the barometer. The barometer tells us what the pressure of the air is, that is, essentially, the weight of air above the barometer. Unfortunately, as we know, there are only too many erratic variations of the weather that cause fluctuations in the barometer. However, if one studies the minutest motions of the barometer for long periods and averages out everything that does not conform to the frequency of the tides, then one can measure the tides of the atmosphere. When this subject was first studied some thirty years ago, it was found that one of the solar tides led to considerably larger fluctuations of the barometer than had been expected. How could this curious behavior be explained? The behavior of the upper atmosphere cannot be channeled as the seas are by a suitably shaped coast line. The only possible explanation was that the atmosphere was in resonance.

## Tidal Resonance

Resonance is an important phenomenon in physics. It refers to the fact that even a small force can become greatly amplified if it is applied repeatedly at just the moment when the oscillation of a body makes it most effective. A repeated push on a swing will make it go quite high, even if the push is gentle, provided it is always applied at the right moment—that is, at the moment when the swing is going in just the direction of the push. In this case, we say that the swing is in resonance with the exciting force, the push. Thus the only explanation of the high atmospheric tide is that the "push" of the tidal forces is applied always just at the right moment to increase a natural oscillation of the atmosphere. One therefore has to look at the natural oscillations of the atmosphere.

It emerged nearly thirty years ago that the atmosphere could be in resonance with the tide-raising forces only if the upper atmosphere has portions much warmer than had been believed at that time, when it had been thought that all the high atmosphere was exceedingly cold. It could be shown, however, that only an atmosphere with a comparatively warm layer high up could resonate with the solar tide and thus lead to the high tides observed. Much more recent work with high-flying balloons and rockets has confirmed what was first discovered as a result of the fluctuations of the barometer, that there is a comparatively warm zone high up in the atmosphere. A very interesting suggestion connected with the atmospheric tides has been made more recently. As we have seen, the tidal fluctuation of the ocean has been slowing down the rotation of the earth so that the length of the day—originally possibly only some eight hours—is now twenty-four hours. Of course, when the length of the day was different, then the tides of the atmosphere occurred with shorter intervals and there can have been no such resonance, no large tide of the atmosphere.

What a curious coincidence, it was suggested, that it should be just in our time that the length of the day was such that there was a resonance! However, it may be no coincidence at all. For it has been shown that, with this resonance and with the daily heating and cooling of the atmosphere that is also due to the sun, a force would be exerted on the earth counteracting the tidal friction of the oceans; the force would tend to keep the length of the day just at its present value, not permitting the ocean tides to lengthen it. If this theory is correct, then it is no coincidence that we have this resonance. On the contrary, the day has probably not lengthened for a long, long time. The idea would be that, although the days grew longer and longer from their original length for many years, when the length of the day reached twenty-four hours—which may have been a long time ago—the curious combination of the resonance of the atmosphere and its daily heating served to keep the day at twenty-four hours, and will go on keeping it at this value for a long time.

# XII.   The Earth: Motion and Magnetism

The whole body of the earth moves in an extraordinarily complicated way when all the small details are considered. The main motions, the daily rotation and the revolution of the earth about the sun in its annual orbit, are well known; but there are many other much smaller motions that also have considerable significance. One that has already been mentioned is the circling of the earth and the moon about their common center of mass. Although the moon does virtually the whole of the moving owing to its much smaller mass, there is some movement of the earth involved in this. Most of the other small motions are due to the fact that the earth is not a sphere, but has a bulge round the equator. The earth is fatter round the equator because the centrifugal force of the daily rotation has stretched the material there. As a result, the equatorial diameter of the earth is some 25 miles longer than the polar diameter. A body of this type, even if it were alone in space, would move in quite a remarkable way.

## Wobble of the Earth's Axis

Owing to the equatorial bulge of the earth, there is a definite axis of figure, the shortest diameter. As long as the body is spinning about this diameter, its motion is quite steady. This can be shown from the theory of the rotation of perfectly rigid bodies. However, if a rigid body of this shape is slightly disturbed so that it spins

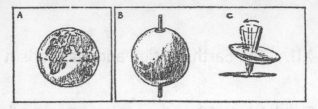

FIG. 49. *The earth is not a true sphere but has a slight bulge around the equator caused by the centrifugal force of its daily rotation. Thus the equatorial diameter is 25 miles longer than the polar diameter. This is not a large difference when we consider the earth's total diameter is 7,920 miles. This may be compared to the motions of a sphere spinning on a shaft with an enlarged bearing; it would produce a slight wobble of the sphere. The equatorial bulge is sufficient to give the earth a slight wobble in its spin. The wobble also follows the motions of a top when nearing the end of its spin.*

not quite about its axis of figure, then a very complex motion results. In this motion the axis of rotation is always at the same distance from the axis of figure; but it moves around it in a period that, in the case of the earth, assuming it to be perfectly rigid, could be worked out to be a little over 300 days. How would we notice such a motion of the earth? For all practical purposes, the direction of the axis of rotation in such a motion would be fixed in space. That is to say, it would always be pointing to the same star, which we may suppose to be our Pole Star. If the axis of rotation moves around the axis of figure, then places on the earth will sometimes be a little nearer to the axis of rotation and sometimes a little farther from it. Accordingly, sometimes the Pole Star will appear, at a fixed place, to be a little higher in the sky and sometimes a little lower. The height of the Pole Star is what we call the geographical latitude. Accordingly, in such a motion of the earth the latitude of every place would fluctuate with a period of some 300 days.

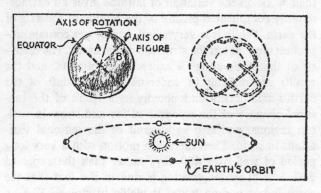

AXIS OF ROTATION

EQUATOR

AXIS OF FIGURE

A

B

SUN

EARTH'S ORBIT

FIG. 50. *In the course of a year the axis of rotation of the earth wanders around the shortest diameter, the axis of figure, and traces out a complex pattern around the pole. The angle between A and B is very much exaggerated in the diagram. Viewed from above the North Pole, the axis of rotation moves about the axis of figure in a very complicated manner.*

For many years this motion, the variation of latitude, was looked for before it was eventually discovered at the end of the last century. The motion was so difficult to discover partly because it was so small and partly because it was much less regular than anticipated. The motion certainly is small. The pole of the axis of rotation of the earth moves only 20 or 30 feet in this curious wobble. That is to say, the latitudes of places on the earth vary by only a small fraction of one second of arc. It was soon found that the motion was so complicated and so irregular that it was desirable to record it exactly. For this purpose a number of international latitude observatories were set up all around the earth. These have now been functioning for many decades, and their work on the variation of latitude gives an extraordinarily complicated picture of the motion of the axis of the earth. While it is very small, it may yet contain important clues about the structure of the earth. The analysis of the observations is exceedingly intricate, and the results are difficult to understand. Some shift of the earth's axis occurs undoubtedly as a result of the seasonal changes of the amounts of ice and snow in various regions, and also as a result of the seasonal variations in wind. Then there is a motion with a very long period of well over 400 days rather than the expected 300 days. This lengthening is due to the fact that the earth is not a rigid body. It yields to stresses like an elastic body. This yielding, and also the damping of the motion, are among the few clues we have about the deep interior of the earth.

## Shift of the Earth's Axis

Another important motion is the so-called precession of the earth's axis. It is well known that the axis of the earth is not at right angles to its plane of motion about the sun, and it is to this inclination that we owe the seasons. In our summer it is the Northern Hemisphere in which the sun is high in the sky; whereas, six months later, the sun is high in the sky in the Southern Hemisphere, and we, in the north, have winter. If the earth were a perfect sphere, then the sun or any other body would be quite unable by gravitational attraction to make the sphere turn in any way, as a sphere is very slippery in a gravitational sense; but the earth has a bulge about the equator. The sun and the moon, by their gravitational attraction, try to pull this equatorial bulge into the plane of the earth's motion about the sun (which is also very nearly the plane of the moon's orbit about the earth). They try to straighten out the earth's axis; they apply a force that tries to diminish its inclination. If the earth were not spinning about its axis, if it did not have its daily rotation, then the forces would soon be successful.

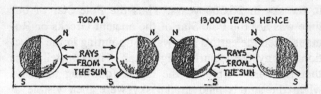

FIG. 51. *Precession of the earth's axis: In 13,000 years the earth's seasons will be reversed, a result of the sun's attraction on the earth's equatorial bulge. In the "today" picture the left-hand figure shows the earth's northern hemisphere turned toward the sun in northern summer; the right-hand figure shows southern-hemisphere summer and northern winter. In the "13,000 years hence" picture the earth's axis has turned through 90 degrees, and the seasons are reversed. At the left is southern summer and at the right northern summer.*

A rotating body tends, however, to react in a curious fashion to forces that try to change its axis of rotation. This is easily seen if one turns a bicycle upside down, resting it on its saddle, spins a wheel and then tries to move the axis of this wheel. It will respond in a most unexpected way by turning at right angles to the direction in which we wish to turn it. These curious forces of spinning bodies form the basis of the spinning top—that favorite toy—and also of the useful gyroscopic compass that has, for many applications, superseded the magnetic compass as an aid to navigation. In the case of the earth, its rotation results in the gravitational pull of sun and moon leading to a turning of the earth's axis about the normal to the plane of the earth's orbit about the sun. This is not a fast rotation; it takes 26,000 years for the earth to get back to where it was. However, it has significant effects: it means that the earth's axis does not always point at the same star, but describes a circle in the sky in 26,000 years. Thus the Pole Star of our time was not the Pole Star of the ancient Greeks or Romans when the earth's axis was not pointing in the direction of any particularly bright star. The constellations that now are visible on the nights following the days when the sun is high in the sky were then visible at a time shifted by a month against that date. And any astronomer who is trying to follow the investigations of the ancient Greeks into astronomy, or the ancient Egyptians or Babylonians, has to make full allowance for the change in the direction of the earth's axis.

## Source of the Earth's Magnetism

We have just referred to the magnetic compass. The fact that this instrument works at all is due to the magnetism of the earth. For hundreds of years people have puzzled as to why this huge body should be magnetic. We know, of course, that certain types of iron can be magnetic; but iron forms a very small part of the outer layers of the earth. Moreover, even if there were enough iron to produce the magnetism, we would still be faced with the question of how it came to be magnetized. In any case, we are now reasonably certain not only that there isn't enough iron about to account for the earth's magnetism, but also that not very far below the surface the temperature becomes so high that even iron ceases to be magnetic.

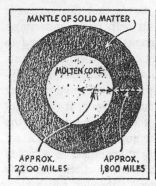

FIG. 52. *It is not very well understood how the earth produces its magnetism. However, it almost certainly is due to the large fluid core which can produce electrical currents of sufficient magnitude to create the earth's magnetic field. The earth's magnetic field extends far out into space, getting weaker and weaker with distance. This magnetic field is of importance to mankind. It controls the compass, so useful for navigation; it modifies the conducting layers in the ionosphere which allow us to send long-distance radio messages; and it helps to protect us from cosmic rays.*

The only other way in which magnetism can be produced is electrically. There are many examples of this in engineering, from the big electromagnets used on some cranes, and the electric motors (which all work on magnetic principles) down to the familiar electric bell in which a contact is broken by magnetic forces. But where can the currents—the huge electric currents required—originate that maintain the earth's magnetic field? The only place one can think of is the liquid core of the earth that extends out from the near center to just over half the radius of the earth. It is known from investigations of earthquake waves that this region is liquid in nature. How can this help us to understand the origins of the electric currents that are required to account for the earth's magnetic field? Electric currents always have to be generated, as, for example, in a dynamo in an electric power station. An essential property of the dynamo is that it has moving parts. It seems not unreasonable to expect that there are motions in the liquid core of the earth. But another very important property of dynamos is that they are made in a highly skilled manner, using wires in which electricity can flow easily and also insulating materials through which electricity cannot flow. On the other hand, the material in the core of the earth is wholly conductive, or so at least we think on the basis of our theories. It is material at very much higher pressure than anything we have in the laboratory, but the physicists feel reasonably happy in ascribing high electrical conductivity to such a material. The question then arises of how we can have a dynamo in a material that is all-conducting and therefore without the interplay of conductors and insulators that makes up the dynamos at electric power stations.

It has turned out that this is a problem of the utmost mathematical complexity, and only quite recently have successful suggestions been made about how such an all-conducting liquid has to move in order to lead to the generation of electrical currents. Once this problem is fully solved, we are still faced with the question of why the fluid of the earth's core moves just in such a way as to lead to the generation of currents and, with it, of a magnetic field. Two suggestions have been made about the origin of these motions. According to one, there is enough radioactive material in the core to produce a certain amount of heat. The only way that this heat can get out is through the whole material being in constant motion like water in a saucepan just before it is boiling. The other suggestion relates to what was mentioned in the earlier part of this chapter, that the earth is going through extremely complicated motions, including the precession of its axis. We know these motions only for the solid mantle of the earth, but the fluid core has some-how to adjust itself to these complex movements of the shell that contains it. In these attempts of the fluid core to follow the mantle, motions of the liquid may quite easily arise; and, conceivably, these may just be the mo-tions that are required to generate the electric currents responsible for the earth's magnetic field.

Some clues are available about all this. There is, first of all, the curious fact that the magnetic poles of the earth are not exactly where the geographical poles are, but are not far away from them either. Why should the magnetic field be almost, but not completely, lined up with the rotation of the earth? Perhaps if we understood more of the motions in the core of the earth we should be nearer to knowing the answer to this question. Next, we have curious indications, found in the last few years by detailed examinations of the magnetism of old rocks, that a long time ago, in certain geological periods, the magnetic field of the earth was different in direction from what it is now. If the origin of the earth's magnetic field is indeed in the fluid core, we may understand how it can have changed over long periods of time, though we are far from a full understanding. But, in any case, this result does speak very much for the theory that the fluid core is responsible for the currents that lead to the magnetic field, and that this is not due to fixed iron rocks.

Enough has been said to indicate how extremely puzzling the earth's magnetic field is. When we wander through space, as we have done in this book, and find, to our surprise, that there are a few features of bodies very far away, such as the stars, that we seem to understand quite well, then it comes as a healthy corrective to any overconfidence that so near at hand as in the center of the earth we have far more questions than answers, and work for many generations of scientists.

# INDEX

Absolute luminosity of stars,
  57–58
  and Hertzsprung-Russell
    diagram, 67 ff.
  –mass relation, 73
  and parallax, 61
  –radius relation, 75
  and size, 64
  from spectrum, 66
  (*See also* Light.)
Aerials,
  and polarization, 85
Ages,
  of galaxies, 43–44, 47–50
  of universe, 37 ff.
Air,
  tides in, 129–32
Alaska,
  Aurora in, 89, 91
Alchemy,
  and universal solvent, 96
American lunar probes, 93
Antarctica,
  Aurora in, 91
Apparent luminosity of stars,
  57–58
  and parallax, 61
  (*See also* Light.)
Artificial satellites,
  orbits of, 115–17

and trapped radiation, 93
  weather, 130
Astronomy, 17 ff.
  ancient, 138
  and Newton's law, 19–20
    (*See also* Newton's Law
    of Gravity.)
  and Olbers' paradox, 27–34
  radio, 88
  and stars, 57–66 ff. (*See
    also* Stars.)
  and velocity-distance law,
    23–25
  (*See also* Cosmology;
    Physics; Space; etc.)
Atmospheric tides, 129–32
Atomic-power stations, 95
Aurora, the, 89–94
Axis of earth,
  shift (precession) of, 136–
    38, 141
  wobble of, 133–36

Baffin Island,
  magnetic pole on, 91
Balloons, high-flying,
  and atmospheric tides, 131
Baltic Sea,
  no tides in, 128, 129

Barometers,
   and atmospheric tides, 130
Bay of Fundy,
   tides in, 125–27
Bicycle wheels,
   axis of rotation of, 137
Binary (double) stars,
   forces between, 121–23
   masses of, 65–66
Black Sea,
   no tides in, 128
Bondi, Hermann, 9–11
Bondi, Mrs. Hermann (Christine Stockman), 10–11
Boston,
   Bondi's lectures in, 11
Bottles, magnetic, 95–96
Brightness,
   of galaxies, and cosmologies, 51–52
   of galaxies, and velocity-distance law, 22 ff.
   of stars and Olbers' paradox, 27 ff.
   of supernovae, 54–55
   (See also Light.)
Bristol Channel,
   tides in, 128

Calcium,
   in cloud dust, 81
Calder Hall atomic-power station, 95
Cambridge,
   Bondi at, 10–11
Cambridge Philosophical Society,
   Bondi in, 11
Canada,
   Aurora in, 89, 91
   tides in Bay of Fundy, 125–27
Carbon,
   in cloud dust, 81
Celestial bodies,
   motion of, 111–20
   (See also Comets; Planets; Stars; etc.)
Center of mass described, 121
Centrifugal force,
   and earth's shape, 133
   and tides, 122–23 ff.
Chinese supernova, 54–55
Clouds in space, 87–88
   composition of, 81
   glowing of, 81–82
   (See also Fog; Gases in space.)
Coal Sack in Milky Way, 79
Color,
   of Aurora, 89–90
   cosmic haze and stellar, 80–81
   and expansion of universe, 21–23 ff.
   and temperature of star surfaces, 61–64, 67 ff.
Comets,
   orbits of, 114, 118
Compasses,
   gyroscopic, 138
   magnetic, 138
Conic sections,
   orbiting in, described, 113

Conservation-of-matter law, 43
Continual creation, 42–46 ff.
Cornell University,
  Bondi at, 11
Cosmic haze, 80–82
  (*See also* Clouds in space;
    Fog.)
Cosmology, 36–55
  and expansion of universe,
    20–34 ff.
  and Olbers' paradox, 27–34
  relativistic, 36–41, 48–50 ff.
  steady-state, 9 ff., 41–46,
    47 ff.
  tests of, 47–55
*Cosmology* (Bondi), 11
Crab Nebula, 55
Creation, continual, 42–46 ff.

Darkness of night sky, 27–34
Days,
  length of, and tides, 132
Density,
  of earth, variation in, 105,
    117
  of stars, 70–71, 77–78
Dimness (*see* Brightness)
Distances,
  and evolution of galaxies,
    51–52
  of stars, measuring, 58–61,
    66
  and velocity of recession,
    23–25
Double (binary) stars,
  forces between, 121–23

masses of, 65–66
Dust in space, 87–88
  composition of, 81
  and polarized starlight, 86
Dynamos,
  and earth's magnetic field,
    140

Earth,
  and gravity, 102, 103–9
    influence with moon, 99 ff.,
    114–15 ff., 121 ff., 128–29
  length of days, 132
  meteors' speed and, 118–19
  moon and, 99 ff., 114–15,
    117
  lunar tides, 121, 123–25,
    128–29
  radiation belts of, 89–94
  shape of, 102, 115–17
    motions due to, 133–38
  shift of axis, 136–38
  source of magnetism, 138–42
  tides, 121–32
  tunnels through, 103–5
  velocity, 119
  wobble of axis, 133–36
Eclipses,
  and deflection of light, 120
  predicted by Newton's law,
    19
Eddington, Sir Arthur S.,
  and mass-luminosity rela-
    tion, 72–73
  and star-center temperature,
    53

Einstein's Theory of Relativity,
and free fall, 107–9
and Newton's theory, 19–20,
107, 114, 120
and relativistic cosmology,
36 ff.
Electricity,
charged particles and Aurora, 91–94
currents in space, 87
and earth's magnetism, 139–
41
Elements,
in cloud dust, 81
origin of, 52–55
(*See also* by name.)
Ellipses,
as orbits, 113–14 ff.
Energy (*see* Heat; Light; Nuclear reactions.)
England,
Aurora in, 89–90
Bondi in, 10–11
English Channel,
tides in, 128
Evolving universe, theory of,
36–41
tests of, 48–50, 51–52, 53,
55
Expanding universe, 20–34 ff.
Explosion in Lemaître's theory, 37

Falling bodies, 105–9, 111
Finite universe described, 36–
37

Fission-type atomic-power stations, 95
Fog, 80
and polarized starlight, 85–
86
(*See also* Clouds in space.)
Free falling, 105–9
Fusion of hydrogen, to helium,
53, 74–77
and aging galaxies, 43
for power stations, 94–96
in Red Giants, 75–77
in White Dwarfs, 77
Fusion-power generating stations, 94, 96

Galaxies, 20–25, 41 ff.
ages of, 47–50
distances of, 21 ff., 51–52
and evolutionary universe,
41, 48–50, 51–52
formation of, 41, 43–46, 52
and Olbers' paradox, 33–34
spectra of, 21–23
and steady-state theory, 43–
46, 50, 51–52
supernovae in, occurrence
of, 54–55
and velocity-distance, law,
23–25
Galileo,
and falling bodies, 105–6,
111
Gases in space, 87–88
and electrical currents, 87
glowing cloud of, 81
magnetic bottles for, 95

Gases in space (*cont'd*)
  and polarized starlight, 86
  and spectra, 21, 64, 80–81
  stars behave as, 70–72, 77
  (*See also* Hydrogen.)
Glare,
  and light polarization, 84–85
Gold, Thomas,
  work with Bondi, 10, 11
Gravitation, 99–131
  and celestial bodies, motion of, 111–19
  and double stars, 121–23
  Einstein's theory of,
    and free fall, 107–9
    and Newton's theory, 19–20, 107, 114, 120
    and relativistic cosmology, 36 ff.
  and inverse square law, 100–3
  and light, 119–20
  Newton's law of, 99–105, 111 ff.
    and Einstein's theory, 19–20, 107, 114, 120
    and tides, 121–32
    and tunnels through earth, 103–5
    and weightlessness, 105–9

Halos,
  and gas clouds, 81
  around moon, 80
Harvard College Observatory,
  Bondi at, 11

Haze, cosmic, 80–82
  (*See also* Clouds in space; Fog.)
Headlights,
  glare of, and polarization, 84–85
Heat,
  and atmospheric tides, 131–32
  and color of stars, 61–64, 67 ff.
  in earth's core, 141
  in home, 63–64
  and nuclear energy generation, 72–74 ff., 94–95
  and origin of elements, 53 ff.
  and size of stars, 64–65, 75
Helium, hydrogen into, 53, 74–77
  and aging galaxies, 43
  for power stations, 94–96
  in Red Giants, 75–77
  in White Dwarfs, 77
Hertzsprung, Prof. E., 67
Hertzsprung-Russell diagrams, 67 ff.
High tides,
  reason for, 125–28
Hoyle, Fred, 10, 11
Hydrogen,
  conversion to helium, 53, 73–77
  and aging galaxies, 43
  for power stations, 94–96
  in Red Giants, 75–77
  in White Dwarfs, 77
  creation of, 42

Hydrogen (*cont'd*)
  gas in space, 79, 88
  origin of elements, 52–53
Hyperbolas,
  as orbits, 113

Iceland,
  Aurora in, 91
*Illustrated London News, The,*
  9
Intrinsic (absolute) luminosity of stars, 57–58
  and Hertzsprung-Russell diagram, 67 ff.
  —mass relation, 73
  and parallax, 61
  —radius relation, 75
  and size, 64
  from spectrum, 66
  (*See also* Light.)
Inverse square law, 100–3
Irish Sea,
  and tidal friction, 129
Iron,
  relation to earth's magnetism, 138–39

Jupiter,
  and sun's mass, 113

Latitude,
  and earth's wobble, 135–36
Laws (*see* Newton's Law of Gravity; etc.)
Lemaître, Abbé,
  evolutionary universe of, 36–41, 55

tests of, 48–50, 51–52, 53
Light,
  from Aurora, 89–90 ff.
  and ages of galaxies, 47–49
  and cosmic haze, 80–82 ff.
  and distances of galaxies, 21 ff., 51
  falling of, 119–20
  luminosity of stars, 57–58
    and Hertzsprung-Russell, diagram, 67 ff.
    —mass relation, 73
    and parallax, 61
    —radius relation, 75
    and size, 64
    from spectrum, 66
  of night sky, 27–34
  pitch of, change in, 22–23
  polarization of, 82–86
  speed of, 23, 28–29, 48
  and star measurements, 57–58 ff., 61–62 ff., 64, 66
  and star structure, 67 ff.
  from supernovae, 54–55
  velocity of recession and spectra, 21–25
*Logic of Scientific Discovery,*
  18
Lowell Lectures,
  Bondi's, 11
Luminosity of stars, 57–58
  and Hertzsprung-Russell diagram, 67 ff.
  —mass relation, 73
  and parallax, 61
  —radius relation, 75
  and size, 64

Luminosity of stars (*cont'd*)
  from spectrum, 66
  (*See also* Light.)
Lunar probes, American, 93
Lunik III,
  moon photography, 117
Lyttleton, Raymond Arthur,
  work with Bondi, 10

Magnetic bottles, 95–96
Magnetic compasses, 138
Magnetic pole, 91, 141
Magnetism,
  to contain high-temperature
    gas, 95–96
  earth's, 97, 138–42
    and Aurora, 91–92 ff.
  in space, 86–87, 96–97
Main sequence stars, 68
  and burning of hydrogen, 75
  and stellar masses, 70
  (*See also* Stars.)
Maine,
  tides in, 128
Mass, center of,
  described, 121
Masses, stellar,
  determining, 65–66
  and Hertzsprung-Russell
    diagram, 70
  —luminosity relation, 73
  of White Dwarfs, 78
Mathematics,
  and continuous creation, 43
  and planetary motion, 113–
    14, 115
  of starlight, 30–33

(*See also* Physics.)
Matter, conservation of, 43
Mercury (planet),
  orbit of, 114
Meteors,
  speed of, 18–19
Methane,
  in cloud dust, 81
Milky Way,
  and clouds in space, 79–80
  and cosmic haze, 81
Moon, our,
  eclipse of sun, 120
  halo around, 80
  and law of gravity, 99 ff.,
    114–15 ff., 121 ff., 137,
    138
  orbit of, 114–15, 117, 137
  position predicted by New-
    ton's law, 19
  and tides, 121, 123–25, 128–
    29
Moons (*see* Satellites)
Motions of earth, 133–38, 141

Neap tides, 125
Nebulae,
  Crab Nebula, 55
  filamentary nebula, 82
  Owl Nebula, 81
New Brunswick,
  tides in Bay of Fundy, 125
Newton's Law of Gravity, 99–
    105, 111 ff.
  and Einstein's theory, 19–
    20, 107, 114, 120

Night sky,
    darkness of, 27–34
North Pole, 91, 141
Nova Scotia,
    tides in Bay of Fundy, 125
Nuclear physics, 52–53 ff., 72,
    73–74 ff.
Nuclear reactions,
    and evolving universe, 37,
        53, 55
    hydrogen to helium, 53, 74–
        77
        and aging galaxies, 43
        for power stations, 94–96
        in Red Giants 75–77
        in White Dwarfs, 77
    and origin of elements, 52–
        55
    and temperature, 53, 55, 72–
        77, 94–95

Ocean (see Tides)
Olbers' paradox, 27–34
Orbits of celestial bodies, 111–
    19
    and sun's force, 111–13
    (See also Earth; Moon, our;
        etc.)
Owl Nebula, 81

Parabolas,
    as orbits, 113
Parallax, trigonometric, 58–61
Particles, electrically charged,
    91–94
Physics,
    and mass of light, 119

nuclear, 52–53 ff., 72, 73–
    74 (See also Nuclear re-
    actions.)
and Olbers' paradox, 29
resonance, 131–32
and steady-state theory, 42
and velocity-distance law,
    23–25
(See also Astronomy; Cos-
    mology; Einstein's Theory
    of Relativity; Newton's
    Law of Gravity.)
Pitch, changes in,
    in light, 22–23
    in sound, 22
Planets,
    motion of, 99, 112–14
    positions of, and Newton's
        law, 19
    (See also by name.)
Polarization,
    of light, 82–85 ff.
    of radio waves, 85
    of starlight, 85–86
Pole star,
    and earth's motion, 134–35,
        138
Poles of earth, 91, 141
Popper, Karl R., 18–19
Population, human,
    illustrates steady-state uni-
        verse, 43
Power stations,
    dynamos in, 140
    fusion-type, 94–96
Precession of earth's axis, 136–
    38, 141

Prisms,
and spectra, 21

Radiation (*see* Heat; Light; Radioactivity)
Radii of stars, 65, 73, 75
Radio astronomy,
and magnetic fields, 88
Radio waves,
from hydrogen, 88
and particles from outer space, 92
polarization of, 85
Radioactivity,
of ash after nuclear fission, 95
in earth's atmosphere, 89–94
in earth's core, 141
Railway train whistle,
pitch of, 22
Recession, velocity of, 22–25
Red Giants,
development, 75–77
on Hertzsprung-Russell diagrams, 68–69, 70
source of elements, 53–54
Red shift of spectrum, 21–23
Relativistic cosmologies, 36–41
testing, 48–50 ff.
Relativity, Einstein's Theory of,
and free fall, 107–9
and Newton's theory, 19–20, 107, 114, 120

and relativistic cosmology, 36 ff.
Repulsion, force of,
and Lemaître's theory, 40–41
Resonance, tidal, 131–32
Roads,
glare on, 84–85
Rockets, high-flying,
and atmospheric tides, 131
and trapped radiation, 93
Rotation of earth, 133, 141
and length of days, 131–32
Royal Astronomical Society,
Bondi in, 11
Royal Society,
Bondi in, 11
Russell, Prof. H. N., 67
Russian satellites, 93
Lunik III, 117
Sputniks, 115–16, 117

Satellites,
artificial, 93, 115–17, 130
orbits of, 114–18
of Saturn, 118
(*See also* by name.)
Saturn,
rings of, 117–18
Science,
methods of, 17–20
(*See also* Cosmology; Mathematics; etc.)
Sea (*see* Tides)
Seasons,
and earth's axis, 136
Severn Bore, 128

Shock waves,
  and glowing clouds, 81–82
Shooting stars,
  speed of, 118–19
Sizes of stars,
  determining, 64–65
  radii, 65, 73, 75
Sky,
  Aurora, the, 89–94
  darkness at night, 27–34
  (*See also* Space; Stars; etc.)
Sleeping,
  in free fall, 107
Solar system, our, 19, 111–
    19 ff.
  (*See also* Moon, our; Sun;
    etc.)
Sound, pitch of,
  and velocity, 22
Space, 79–88
  cosmic haze in, 80–82
  electrical currents in, 87–88
  magnetism in, 96–97
  particles from, 92 ff.
  and polarized light, 82–86
  travel, 94, 107, 108
  (*See also* Galaxies; Stars;
    etc.)
Spectra, 21
  cosmic haze and stellar, 80–
    81
  and distances of stars, 66
  red shift of, 21–23
  and temperatures of stars,
    61–64
Speed (*see* Velocity)

Spring tides, 125
Sputniks,
  and earth's figure, 115–16,
    117
Stars, 57–78
  color of, 61–64, 67 ff., 80–
    81
  and darkness at night, 27–
    34
  double, 65–66, 121–23
  and fall of light, 120
  and Hertzsprung-Russell
    diagrams, 67–70
  magnetic fields of, 96
  masses of, 65–66
    and Hertzsprung-Russell
      diagram, 70
    and luminosity, 73
    of White Dwarfs, 78
  mathematics of starlight,
    30–32
  and origin of elements, 53–
    55
  parallaxes of, 58–61
  polarized starlight, 85–86
  Red Giants, 53–54, 68–69,
    70, 75–77
  shooting, speed of, 118–19
  sizes of, 64–65, 73, 75
  structure of, 70–78
  White Dwarfs, 69, 70, 75–78
  (*See also* Galaxies; Sun;
    etc.)
Steady-state theory, 41–46
  Bondi and, 9, 10, 11
  tests of, 47, 50, 51–52, 53

Stockman, Christine Mary, 10–11

Suffocation,
in free fall, 107

Sun,
density of, 70–71
depth of, 73
and falling of light, 120
and law of gravity, 99, 111–14 ff., 123–25, 131, 136–38
magnetic field of, 96
as main-sequence star, 68
mass of, 113
and shift of earth's axis, 136–38
spectrum of, 21
sunspots, 92, 94, 96
and tides, 123–25, 131, 132

Sunspots, 92, 94, 96

Supernovae, 54–55

TV aerials,
and polarization, 85

Temperature,
and atmospheric tides, 131–32
and color of stars, 61–64, 67 ff.
in earth's core, 141
and energy generation, 72–74 ff., 94–95
and origin of elements, 53 ff.
and sizes of stars, 64–65, 75

Tests in cosmology, 47–55

Theories,
of cosmology, 35–55

Einstein's (see Einstein's Theory of Relativity)
of evolving universe, 36–41, 48–50 ff.
Newton's (see Newton's Law of Gravity)

Olbers' paradox, 27–34
and scientific method, 17–19
of steady-state universe, 41–46, 47 ff.

Tidal friction, 128–29

Tidal resonance, 131–32

Tides, 121–32
atmospheric, 129–32
high, reasons for, 125–28
resonance of, 131–32
sun vs. moon, 123–25

Tiros I, 130

Train whistle,
pitch of, 22

Trapped particles, 92–94

Tunnels,
through earth, 103–5

Twins,
analogy with galaxies' ages, 49

Uniformity of universe,
and cosmological theories, 36, 42
and expansion, 24–25, 36

Universal solvent,
search for, 96

Universe,
evolving, theory of, 36–41, 48–50 ff.

Universe (*cont'd*)
  expansion of, 20–34 ff.
  finite, 36–37
  steady-state theory of, 9 ff.,
    41–46, 47 ff.
  uniformity of, 24–25, 36, 42
Uranium,
  for power station, 95

Vanguard satellite,
  and earth's figure, 117
Velocity,
  of meteors, 118–19
  of recession, 22–25
Very High Frequency aerials,
  and polarization, 85
Violet,
  shift toward, 23

Water,
  level of (*see* Tides)
  pouring in free fall, 106–7
Weight,
  and gravitation, 108
  (*See also* Density; Masses,
    stellar; Weightlessness.)
Weightlessness, 105–9
Whistles,
  pitch of train, 22
White Dwarfs,
  development of, 75–78
  on Hertzsprung-Russell dia-
    grams, 69, 70
Wobble of earth's axis, 133–36

# SCIENCE STUDY SERIES

BATTAN, LOUIS J. *The Nature of Violent Storms,* S 19
    *Radar Observes the Weather,* S 24
    *Cloud Physics and Cloud Seeding,* S 29

BENADE, ARTHUR H. *Horns, Strings, and Harmony,* S 11

BITTER, FRANCIS *Magnets: The Education of a Physicist,* S 2

BONDI, HERMANN *The Universe at Large,* S 14

BOYS, SIR CHARLES VERNON *Soap Bubbles and the Forces Which Mould Them,* S 3

BROWN, SANBORN C. *Count Rumford,* S 28

COHEN, I. BERNARD *The Birth of a New Physics,* S 10

DAVIS, KENNETH S., and DAY, JOHN ARTHUR *Water: The Mirror of Science,* S 18

DUBOS, RENÉ *Pasteur and Modern Science,* S 15

FINK, DONALD G., and LUTYENS, DAVID M. *The Physics of Television,* S 8

GALAMBOS, ROBERT *Nerves and Muscles,* S 25

GAMOW, GEORGE *Gravity,* S 22

GRIFFIN, DONALD R. *Echoes of Bats and Men,* S 4

HOLDEN, ALAN, and SINGER, PHYLIS *Crystals and Crystal Growing,* S 7

HUGHES, DONALD J. *The Neutron Story,* S 1

HURLEY, PATRICK M. *How Old Is the Earth?* S 5

JAFFE, BERNARD *Michelson and the Speed of Light,* S 13

KOESTLER, ARTHUR *The Watershed: A Biography of Johannes Kepler,* S 16

LITTAUER, RAPHAEL, and WILSON, ROBERT R. *Accelerators: Machines of Nuclear Physics,* S 17

MACDONALD, D. K. C. *Near Zero: The Physics of Low Temperature,* S 20

OVENDEN, MICHAEL W. *Life in the Universe,* S 23

PAGE, ROBERT MORRIS *The Origin of Radar,* S 26

ROMER, ALFRED *The Restless Atom,* S 12

SANDFORT, JOHN F. *Heat Engines,* S 27

SHAPIRO, ASCHER H. *Shape and Flow: The Fluid Dynamics of Drag,* S 21

VAN BERGEIJK, WILLEM A.; PIERCE, JOHN R.; DAVID, EDWARD E., JR. *Waves and the Ear,* S 9

WEAVER, WARREN *Lady Luck: The Theory of Probability,* S 30

WEISSKOPF, VICTOR F. *Knowledge and Wonder: The Natural World as Man Knows It,* S 31